A Greener Life

Dedicated to Ada Rose

LAURENCE KING

First published in Great Britain in 2021 by Laurence King Publishing
an imprint of The Orion Publishing Group Ltd
Carmelite House, 50 Victoria Embankment
London EC4Y 0DZ

An Hachette UK Company

10 9 8 7 6 5 4 3 2 1

A CIP catalogue record for this book is
available from the British Library.

ISBN 978-085782-893-4

Printed in China by C&C Offset Printing Co. Ltd.

Laurence King Publishing is committed to ethical
and sustainable production. We are proud participants of
The Book Chain Project
bookchainproject.com

BOOK CHAIN PROJECT

www.laurenceking.com
www.orionbooks.co.uk

Discover the joy of mindful
and sustainable gardening

A Greener Life

Laurence King Publishing

Jack Wallington

Contents

Introduction

Life on Littlebury Road

In 2014, my life changed when my partner Chris and I, along with our cat Rumbles, saved enough of a deposit to buy the small, one-bed, ground-floor flat we'd been renting for six years in the heart of London. On the site of an old Victorian plant nursery, it had a small patio with a narrow side return, tiny compared to most suburban or rural gardens, but in London we were the lucky ones. Many of our friends still rented or had balconies as their only outside space.

Somewhere between education, partying, a career and fighting to get on the property ladder, I felt I'd lost my way. In fact, I had never really found it. My work was stressful. I struggled to sleep and being available 24/7 on email and social media set my heart racing. My physical health suffered; I was regularly ill. I spent the majority of my time inside or squashed together with other passengers on my daily commute. I thought the feeling of dissatisfaction was normal, to be waited out until retirement.

The turning point was the day Chris and I planted the first plants and bulbs in our new garden to celebrate it being ours. Burying the roots in the soil and then watching Rumbles playfully trying to dig them back up, my worries briefly melted away, and a spark of happiness ignited.

Childhood memories trickled back: of sowing tomato and nasturtium seeds and taking cacti cuttings to sell for pocket money. I was excited to see the space I was creating grow and change over the coming months and years. Obsessively I filled the garden with exciting plants to learn how their quirky foliage and striking flowers grew.

It took a long time before I realised what was happening to me. I was better able to deflect stresses and anxieties, and apparently insurmountable problems at work felt insignificant compared to what awaited back in the garden. Life, all life, the thing I had loved as a boy, that had been around me all along, was helping my world make sense.

I had euphoric moments when discovering other gardens and visiting the countryside. I began to feel connected to something bigger than me, and that somehow the things I planted and cared for were making a real contribution. The more I planted in the garden, the more insects and birds visited.

Inviting nature back into my life gave a peace I hadn't experienced for thirty years, and opened my eyes to the responsibility I had to the ecosystem I was nurturing.

Learning what it means to be a gardener

Our garden is a funny little space, overlooked by at least eleven other homes. Planes on their way to Heathrow roar overhead every few minutes and sirens on the nearby high street can be heard. Despite this, it always seems to be a peaceful sanctuary.

As plant and wildlife numbers rocketed I realised what I was doing didn't feel like gardening in the ordinary sense. It felt urgent and important. I didn't understand why until I noticed certain things: how I'd pay attention to the seasons; that a new plant brought a different insect; how certain plant colours and textures transformed the feel of the space. I protected spider webs in autumn (helping me to overcome my arachnophobia – up to a point) because they caught aphids and mosquitoes, and looked pretty covered in dew.

Yet when people think of the word gardener, images of mowing lawns, clipping hedges or digging come to mind. To me, being a gardener is much more than that. It's about heart, mind and soul, a way of thinking and approaching life. A gardener doesn't need a garden, they simply need to be interested in the living world around them, to understand how everything grows together, plants and wildlife, an ecosystem in which we also belong.

Freedom to grow

With 55 per cent of the world's 7.8 billion people living in urban areas (83 per cent in the UK), lack of personal outdoor space is the reality of our time. For those without a garden there are opportunities to get stuck in thanks to community gardens and allotments. My 5m × 6m (16 × 20ft) patio is largely unsuitable for edibles because of the amount of shade, so I started growing vegetables properly in a tiny, raised bed in our local Eden community garden, giving me a number of meals and a determination to reconnect with what we ate.

In 2015 I applied for allotments locally, to be met with twenty-seven-year waiting lists. Eventually I struck lucky further afield on the outskirts of the city, coincidentally in the London suburb of Wallington. Eleven km (7 miles) and two train rides away but four times the size of our garden, it was vast, and I was in love. Here I grew vegetables, fruit, herbs and cut flowers. Finally, I felt free to be me.

Gardening and ecology

Though we have known about habitat destruction, animal extinction and climate change for decades, we have hastened rather than halted it. The Living Planet Report 2020 showed a 68 per cent decrease in population sizes of mammals, birds, amphibians, reptiles and fish between 1970 and 2016, while exhausted natural resources and violent weather systems already impact our lives.

Gardening alone can't save the planet, but if we all look at ways to grow organically and nurture diverse wildlife, it can make a contribution. Too much land has been turned over to livestock and agriculture: fields filled with single-plant crop monocultures and smothered in insecticides. Every garden, park and allotment is a precious oasis for wildlife living on the edge of extinction.

Steps towards a greener life

I began studying horticulture with the Royal Horticultural Society and Royal Botanic Garden Edinburgh, leading to me quitting my office job. I decided to dedicate my life instead to conservation while sharing the health benefits of nature and gardens with others. Now, as a landscape designer and writer, I create beautiful gardens full of wildlife and share what I learn through that process.

This book holds the essential tips I've learned from my personal and professional journey to help you make the most of your outdoor space, to benefit both yourself and nature. It will teach you the fundamentals of how to build an ecosystem that is loved by wildlife and I hope it will also help you appreciate our place within that ecosystem.

For those affected by stress and anxiety, I hope this book helps you to cope and encourages a connection with nature, which has helped me immensely. Gardening can't eliminate these strains from our lives, they are part of who we are, but it can provide a permanent thread to find yourself again, when you need it.

Allow yourself to fail

Importantly, I want this book to reassure you that it's ok if things go wrong, that it's fine to make mistakes and that no one in the world can possibly know everything about gardening and nature. That's a good thing, because the joy of the natural world is not in perfection, or knowing it all, but in learning and discovering. Gardening is about admitting we don't have all the answers but being willing to pick up the seed packet regardless.

One
Living green

From the beginning I wanted an organic, wildlife-friendly garden using sensible materials. But as an artist and designer, I didn't want to sacrifice creativity. Good design makes a space usable and comfortable, while art invites deep thought and conveys the way other people see the world. I wanted to prove to myself that planet-friendly gardens and designed gardens could meet in the middle.

Our garden took on a tropical slant as I was drawn to quirky leaves of *Canna*, *Ricinus* and *Schefflera*, nestling them among local species to create an oasis of pink and purple exotica set against London's terracotta brickwork and grey concrete.

As our garden changed, I knew I was changing. Something had woken inside me that grew with our garden. My increasing awareness of the plants around us, at home and on our streets, helped me see nature's purity and that connection made me stronger to face each day. Gardening was turned on its head: I wasn't helping the garden, it was helping me, leading me towards a greener life.

How gardening changes you

Feeling surrounded by plants and wildlife is, in many respects, similar to the way our ancestors would have lived for hundreds of thousands of years. The period in which we have lived in modern homes, removed from nature, is but a pinprick on humanity's timeline. Wherever I grow something I feel I belong. It's no surprise that this feeling is strongest in our garden because it's the space I've given the most time and thought.

Building a connection with your garden

This sense of belonging, or connectedness, is created by a series of physical and psychological touch points that usually make us feel happy and secure, such as a hug, laughter with friends over dinner, love for a partner. The strongest connections are built through nurture and care.

Simple actions in the garden help our sense of belonging too: planting a bulb is itself a small connection with the earth, as is hearing the joyful sound of birdsong. Rather than a series of chores, gardening can be a practice of constant care, and reward us for it.

At times I feel so closely attached to our garden that even when I'm away, I need only think of it – Have pond skaters arrived? What vegetables shall I grow this year? – and my worst stresses and worries can subside. The garden is a constant daydream to tap into for support.

It's also fun, which helps. Gardens are enjoyable to plan and nurture, but it's the many actions, experiences and memories, creating thousands of tiny connections over time, that bind us to our gardens.

Finding a purpose

Caring for anything, whether it's a person, a plant or an animal, is an expression of empathy, an understanding of what that other life is going through and needs. To be able to help is fulfilling – it makes us feel good. The lockdowns imposed during the Covid-19 pandemic highlighted just how essential nature is to our wellbeing as people sought to reconnect with it in whatever way they could.

My garden and allotment provided me with a much-needed respite during that time, and I've reflected on how they always repay me tenfold for any attention I give them. Biting into a homegrown apple, spotting a combination of plants flowering as hoped or giving birds a place to nest is rewarding, the garden throwing a connection back at me.

Nature has always put life into perspective for me. Feeling responsible

for the life in our garden has been a healthy antidote to my stress and anxiety, and this was certainly the case throughout the pandemic. Treating our garden as more than just an outdoor living space has brought nature's ability to instil wellbeing to our backdoor; and I can even find it indoors thanks to my houseplants.

Of course, it's not just humans who are connected to gardens. They contain whole ecosystems, a matrix of relationships between all life: plants, fungi, worms, insects, birds, animals. Remove one link, such as pollinating insects, and the entire network unravels.

We are better for being connected to the ecosystem and it to us. This connection gives us something we all seek: a purpose.

Above, left Dead-heading *Dahlia* 'Rothesay Rose' to encourage more flowers.
Above, right Common carder bee, *Bombus pascuorum*, feeding on *Symphyotrichum novae-angliae* 'Violetta'.

You are key to a planet-friendly garden

As I've grown with our garden, I've increasingly roamed the countryside too, drawn to seeing wildflowers and insects in their natural habitat, such as the Pasque Flower (*Pulsatilla vulgaris*) and common blue butterflies (*Polyommatus icarus*). Coming home each time to our garden I soon realised that the only difference between it and a wild space is me. Leave a garden to its own devices and nature takes over. Instead, my regular pottering has shaped ours in the same way as a bird builds a nest.

Helping or hindering wildlife is our choice

Humans are curious creatures, so similar to other animals in many respects, and yet so different. Our ability to care for and nurture a wide range of living things, and to be creative at the same time, is one of the gifts to set us apart.

We can be destructive too: well over 50 per cent of the world's forests no longer exist because we've cut them down. Industrial agriculture using insecticides turns fields into black holes for wildlife, and plastic litters our soil and oceans. Habitats for wild creatures and plants are vanishing – many will soon be gone. And even if we aren't directly contributing to those extinctions, our lack of action plays a role.

Increase plant diversity

Gardens are a great place to start helping. From the beginning I grew plants that I knew would add a food source for wildlife, an astrantia for hoverflies in summer here, a hellebore for bumblebees in winter there. Sure enough, the insects arrived, often drawn to flowers like magnets the second I'd planted them. It's amazing how fast insects find flowers. The more I planted with this mindset, the more wildlife arrived and the more beautiful the garden became.

Gardens can become very diverse ecosystems with our assistance, because we can increase the range of plants and habitats in relatively small spaces. Left to their own devices, gardens will certainly turn back into beneficial wild spaces, but to fewer species. We need to be there to prevent a shrub shading out a smaller plant, to water something struggling in drought or to dead-head plants for longer flowering seasons.

Our role in the garden is to steer it into being the best it can be for wildlife while using our creative flair to do so in a way that is also best for us.

Top Exotic and regionally indigenous plants all serve some purpose for wildlife and I've jumbled them together to ensure the greatest diversity.
Bottom Male *Polyommatus icarus*, common blue butterfly, feeding on common bugloss, *Anchusa officinalis*.

Nine steps to a greener gardening life

These principles transformed my garden into a space that not only helped me but wildlife and the planet as well.

1 **Don't use insecticides:** one squirt can kill thousands of different insects, including beneficial ones, throwing your garden's ecosystem out of whack. There are two main types of insecticide: systemic, which soaks into a plant and stays active, killing for weeks or months; and contact, which suffocates insects before being washed away. Systemic is the worst, but neither is needed.

2 **Don't use weedkiller:** weeds are unwanted plants, usually because we don't like their look and they spread seemingly uncontrollably. Understanding how they grow removes the need for weedkiller. I hoe and hand fork them out or starve them of light with a cover of card, weed-suppressant matting or compost mulch.

3 **Use natural fertilisers:** seaweed, free-range chicken manure pellets and homemade compost (see p.94–95) are excellent, removing the need for chemical fertilisers.

4 **Release and feed the soil:** soil holds more life within it than lives above it. But this only works if the soil isn't paved over and has plants growing in it, allowing plant material to decompose and be absorbed into it. Worms and microorganisms feed on the plant material and turn it into nutrients.

5 **Banish plastic:** there is too much waste plastic polluting the planet and we all need to reduce the amount we use. Gardening is filled with plastic from pots to compost bags, making it hard to avoid, but it is possible. Reuse the pots you have to keep them from landfill and stop buying new ones. For raising seedlings I love peat-free fibre pots and soil blockers, even toilet rolls can be used (see p.38)! Bamboo-based pots and terracotta pots are great for larger plants.

6 **Reduce transport miles:** grow your own plants, veggies and cut flowers from seed, which release far less atmospheric carbon in transport and packaging than bought plants.

7 **Make your own compost:** this is one of the best things you can do to be planet-friendly. Ensure an even mix of green and brown waste, turning it a couple of times a year, and use an open bin to welcome wildlife.

8 **Go peat-free:** peat comes from peat bogs, which are a natural habitat for many species of plant and animal; they are also one of the biggest stores of carbon thanks to the anaerobic conditions (lacking oxygen) within them. Digging up peat releases huge amounts of carbon into the atmosphere, exposing it to oxygen and forming CO_2. I only use peat-free compost. The brands can vary in nutrient value, but I find this is always remedied by adjusting the amount of fertiliser up or down to suit.

9 **Be water wise:** water is a precious commodity. Collect rainwater in tanks and use plants that won't need additional watering in your garden after the first year. For some plants, especially perennials and annuals, a slight ridge of soil helps hold water around the plant, stopping wasteful runoff. Creating larger dips and ponds in your garden can help excess water drain into the soil and prevent flooding.

Focusing on organic gardening

Gardening organically sounds difficult, I know, but if you follow the principles on pages 18–19 you will find that's exactly what you are doing. I have found that growing organically has brought me closer to my garden. By understanding how everything is connected, you learn why chemicals aren't needed. It's tempting to reach for the bug spray when a plant you've poured your hopes and efforts into is covered in nibbling caterpillars, but if you forgo these quick-fix sprays your garden's wildlife will eventually balance itself out. When it does, you'll wonder why you used the sprays in the first place.

Bad insects are food for the good

Bothersome aphids, caterpillars, slugs and other suckers and nibblers are food to wildlife we do like, such as birds, frogs, small mammals and hoverflies. By using insecticides not only do we risk killing the good guys, we remove their food and a reason for them to patrol our gardens in the first place.

Sadly, with agricultural land full of systemic insecticides and gardens too, there are fewer and fewer places for insects to live, which means the birds, bats and other mammals that feed on those vanished insects vanish with them. Everything is connected and insecticides sever every connection.

Beware of hidden poisons

In recent years I've suspected the plants I buy from garden centres or nurseries are pumped full of these poisons, one of the main reasons I now propagate more of my own plants (pp.39–43). Most disturbing are the times I see many bodies of fuzzy bumble and solitary bees in my garden – evidence that someone nearby has sprayed their garden. It's upsetting to see these little creatures that I've been encouraging and getting to know, lying dead.

Controlling pests organically

At times pests can outnumber the wildlife that eat them, particularly when you first go organic, before the garden's ecosystem has rebalanced. Here are some techniques to help reduce their numbers:

+ **Use your hands:** aphids can be wiped off or squished with your fingers, quickly reducing the population. The less squeamish can treat caterpillars and asparagus beetle the same way.
+ **Hose:** aphids on firm stems of roses or broad beans can be washed off gently with a hose.

- **Shake them off:** vine weevil, lily and rosemary beetle can be shaken off the plant on to a white sheet spread beneath to catch and spot them, and dispatched.
- **Biological control:** you can boost your good insect numbers by buying extra ladybirds to eat aphids, microscopic wasps to kill mealybugs and nematodes for various uses. All are available online. Nematodes are microscopic soil organisms that can be mixed in watering cans and kill slugs and the ground-dwelling larvae of crane flies (leatherjackets) and vine weevils.
- **Move them:** I don't kill caterpillars or snails anymore. Instead, I move them somewhere else in a box or jar. I transport snails about half a mile down the road to a wild spot where they won't find their way back, because they have a homing range of 20m (65ft).

Make your own natural fertiliser
You can make your own fertiliser using nutrients from comfrey (*Symphytum*), a deep-rooted perennial, or stinging nettles (*Urtica dioica*). Comfrey is potash rich, encouraging flower and fruit production, while nettles are nitrogen rich, encouraging leaf growth.

1 Grow *Symphytum* × *uplandicum* 'Bocking 14', a sterile comfrey that won't set seed and therefore must be bought as a plant. Cut leaves and stems when the plant is about 50cm (20in) tall and bushy (discard any flowers, they don't hold much nutrient).
2 Fill a 10-litre (2½-gallon) bucket with 1 kg (2lb) of leaves and stems and top up with water.
3 Cover and leave for a 4–6 weeks – prepare for a stench!
4 The resulting liquid is rich fertiliser for flowers and fruit that doesn't need diluting. Nettle fertiliser is made in the same way but takes only 2 weeks to be ready and does need diluting, at 1 part nettle solution to 10 parts water.

Two
Getting started

For me, the best part of gardening is not the end result but the process: knowing how to plant, care for and gently steer your garden to be the best it can be. Everyone can learn these skills and techniques by giving it a go.

I don't see activities in the garden as chores but as an excuse to be outside, spending time among the plants and bees. Whether I'm planting crocus bulbs in autumn, watching tomato seeds I've sown in spring germinate or shaping an apple tree in summer, these gentle tweaks over time give me a role and a reason to get up each day.

An increasing number of scientific studies prove that gardening is good for our physical and mental wellbeing, but I don't need to read any to already know it is true. Planting, snipping and lifting are all good forms of exercise and the process of gardening through the seasons is mindful in a variety of ways. From planning a flower-filled future, to quietly weeding, it's learning the techniques of gardening that has had the greatest impact on our garden, and me.

Easy planning for better results

I don't like planning our garden too much, otherwise it feels like a chore. But there are four secrets to success I come back to time and again to make the best of our garden and other people's.

Observe what's happening

I spend more time observing how plants grow than I spend doing anything else in the garden. Observing a garden teaches us to understand what will happen in the future by learning from the past, and it gives us time to make informed changes.

For me, the time spent in observation is when I find gardening the most rewarding and mindful. Observation sparks a series of mental processes:

✛ **Watching:** finding joy or interest in seeing the live ecosystem at work
✛ **Understanding:** discovering how plants grow, which plants wildlife species prefer, and so on
✛ **Remembering:** what did you do in the past and what were its effects?
✛ **Planning:** imagining the future and how your actions will shape it

Draw a garden plan

Before I did anything in our garden I drew a rough pencil sketch of the shape of it and marked on where I thought each plant should go, which helped me plan the best combinations. Every year or so I revisit this plan with new ideas for changes before I make them.

Draw the outline of your garden on gridded paper or on a computer using an easy scale, such as 1cm:1m or 1cm:50cm/1in:5ft (see page 49). Keeping

to scale is important for preventing mistakes in real life later – nothing is worse than finding your snazzy new shed doesn't fit! Don't waste time making it look fancy; keeping it simple is the best way to make it legible and easy to update.

Mark on the drawing the exact positions of any large trees and shrubs that are already there, as well as your house and other structures (existing or planned) such as a greenhouse, paths, patios and raised beds.

Finally, mark the plants you'd like, using circles to denote the plants at their estimated final size to give you the correct spacing. If your garden is large, you might need to do this in groups of, say, five plants rather than individually, for speed. The plan helps you think about the conditions of different areas, such as sun and shade, as well as the spacing of plants. It's worth a quick vertical sketch to check height as well.

Organise seasonal tasks

Rather than relying on other people's guides, make your own basic list of what to do in your garden across the year – because every garden is different. I have a very basic spreadsheet with notes of what needs doing by month in our garden and allotment. Rather than planning it all in one go, each year I've made notes of what I've done and when, giving me a comprehensive list over time.

But the easiest way I do this is to store seed packets by the month when they should be sown (it tells you when on the packet). That way, I don't need to remember everything, I just look in the seed box a couple of times a month to see what I need to do.

Write weekly to do lists

This point sounds so obvious you could be forgiven for wondering why I've included it, but keeping a to do list on my smartphone is my essential form of planning. I check it and update it every day, making sure my list is never more than five to ten points long. If it is, I either make a concerted effort to work through it or delete the bottom tasks – if they were so important I'd have done them already. I can always add them back on later.

What do you want from your garden?

It's fully possible to create a beautiful garden that encourages a sense of wellbeing while also being environmentally and wildlife-friendly. Think what you'd like from the garden – time spent with nature, quiet alone time, socialising – and ways to achieve this, such as seating, a new planting area or pot plants.

✛ **A spot to sit in:** choosing where to sit to relax or socialise is an important starting point. Do you want sun or shade? What will the view from the seats be? Do you want to be in the open to feel free and spacious, or in a sheltered private spot to feel enclosed and safe? Do you want to chat on sofas, recline on loungers or perch on a bench? We opted for comfortable rocking chairs in our space.

✛ **A space for outdoor dining:** if you have the space, natural wood or long-lasting metal table sets are best for the environment and look timeless – and are handy for use as an outdoor desk too. Do you need a BBQ and outdoor kitchen area or are you close enough to the kitchen inside?

✛ **A route to reflection:** I love paths for their sense of journey. I find walking along them deep in thought while looking at plants and insects one of the underrated joys of the outdoors. Not much space is needed for a path; in our garden one path is only 2m (6½ft) long but it holds the same power for generating contemplative thought.

✛ **A room with a view:** always consider the view from the house to the garden because you'll see it multiple times each day. Think of it like a living painting, your most valuable artwork.

✛ **A play area for children:** garden space can be in short supply in small to medium gardens, making it beneficial to dedicate an area for trampolines, swings or treehouses. This gives everyone personal space to relax without the garden being overrun by toys.

✛ **A place for storage:** reduce clutter with the right size cupboard or shed.

Opposite A quiet seating area to catch evening sun, surrounded by waist-high grasses *Calamagrostis brachytricha* and *Pennisetum* 'Fairy Tails'.

Once you've decided on the main usable areas you need, you have a structure to make smarter style and material choices, planning things in an intelligent way.

✣ **Create a mood:** creating mood is the unspoken secret of memorable gardens. Usually it's colour, shape, texture and pattern that change the mood. Lots of bright colours can be jolly and nurture happiness, all-white gardens can appear ethereal, smart or formal, giving a sense of reassurance; and texture-led green foliage gardens generate calm and peace. In our garden, I use pinks and purples for fun and a sense of warmth even on a cold day, but the overall colour palette is muted thanks to a high percentage of foliage for shape and texture, which keeps it feeling calming and relaxed; it always brings me back down to earth.

✣ **Use sustainable materials:** choose permeable materials that let water drain through, like wood decking, gravel, brick, setts and cobbles, or lay smaller slabs without the use of cement. Or, if you can't use the aforementioned materials, at least ensure water runs into planting areas. Buy materials as locally as possible to reduce transportation, and where possible use reclaimed and recycled materials.

✣ **Plan the best planting zones:** plants need space and I always look to create the biggest planting area possible. Most people make the mistake of planting in narrow strips down the edges of walls and fences (the driest spots), where little fits or grows happily except climbers. If you can, aim for beds with a minimum depth of 1.5–2m (5–7ft). Any less and you'll struggle to grow everything you need.

✣ **Use fewer but larger pots:** for easier long-term container planting, always go for large pots of 30cm (12in) diameter or more. Small pots dry out quickly and offer too little root space, making your life and the plant's miserable.

Opposite, clockwise from top left *Perovskia* 'Blue Spire'; *Begonia palmata* 'Tie Dye'; *Dahlia* 'Bishop of Canterbury'; *Clematis* 'Dutch Sky', *Dryopteris wallichiana, Hydrangea* 'Little Lime' and *Hakonechloa macra.*

Essential concepts

There are a number of things about gardening that are only truly possible to understand by getting stuck in and doing them, learning from mistakes and successes. Here are a few.

✛ **Don't just choose familiar plants:** they could be wrong for your garden. Instead, research the conditions in areas of your garden first (e.g. sun, shade, soil type and water) and choose plants that match by habitat. This may take a bit more time at first but will make for happier plants.

✛ **Making a garden takes time:** using young plants is better than using mature ones because it's cheaper, reduces transport and, importantly, allows plants to settle in better, often growing stronger. I encourage everyone to enjoy this process of growth and change. It can be a year or two before the garden starts to look how you imagined, but this change is so rewarding. Low-cost annuals and bulbs can fill gaps in early years.

✛ **Water and drainage are key:** in an ideal world there would be a magic formula for how much water to give a plant, but that's impossible because every plant is affected differently by conditions such as temperature, humidity, wind and light. I focus on the soil or compost. Most plants like soil to be slightly moist, like a damp sponge, but not soaking wet. The best way to learn is by practising on a few plants that have different water requirements, e.g. one that prefers drier conditions with free-draining soil and infrequent watering, such as a succulent, and one preferring water-retentive, damp soil, such as a fern. Even the most experienced gardeners struggle with watering from time to time; getting it right is one of the hardest parts of gardening, so don't worry if there are some casualties along the way!

✛ **The right light is crucial for growing success:** it can be hard to work out the different light levels plants need when terms like 'dappled shade' or 'part-sun' seem to suggest the same thing. In our garden I watched where the light fell in each month of the year, changing with the height of the sun. I noted solid obstacles like fences as well as

Opposite, clockwise from top left
Our garden has full sun on the left and full shade on the right by the fence; Calamagrostis brachytricha can tolerate part shade, allowing Symphyotrichum 'Little Carlow' to tumble into it; gardens can take years to become established.

those like deciduous shrubs that allow more light in during winter when their leaves drop. Full or direct sun is exactly that, nothing sits between the sun and the plant. Full shade is the opposite, the plant receiving no direct sunlight at all. Part-shade means mostly direct sun with 4–6 hours of shade, and part-sun the opposite, mostly full shade with 4–6 hours of direct sun.

✛ **Not all plants like cold weather:** every plant has a different tolerance for cold,

wet weather, called 'hardiness'. Except those stated as tender (which means they can't survive below freezing), I've tested all outdoor plants in this book to -8°C (17°F), and most can withstand lower temperatures. Exceptions that

Above, left A hand hoe makes light work of weeds in raised beds and around plants that could be accidentally damaged by a regular hoe, such as onions and asparagus.
Above, right Some plants that flower from leaf joins (called nodes) high on the stems can have spent flowers cut off at the join to encourage more, such as this *Dahlia*.

struggle below -5°C (23°F) are Canna, Dahlia, Verbena bonariensis, some Salvia and tender Agapanthus. When sourcing plants, look for hardiness ratings. In the UK, a rating of H3 to H7 indicates an increasing tolerance of freezing temperatures. In the USA it's the reverse: hardiness zones of Z9 or lower indicates increasing tolerance. Note your area's lowest temperature and use plants that can survive.

+ **Feed your soil for stronger plants:** the health of your plants depends entirely on the health of your soil. Healthy soil has a structure with soil particles held together in clumps, with tiny gaps for air and water around them and high amounts of organic matter, mainly decomposing plants and animal excrement. This is broken down by fungi and other soil organisms, releasing nutrients in a form that plant roots can absorb called humus, which is broken-down organic matter. Soil organisms like worms, woodlice and microscopic nematodes help maintain the structure of soil because humus binds soil particles and the small channels they dig create cavities for water, air and roots. As do plant roots, which have their own seasonal pattern of dying back and growing underground, forming cavities and creating decomposing plant matter. The secret to keeping the cycle going is a good layer of new organic matter each year, which I achieve by leaving leaves and dead plants on the soil and by adding a good 5–7cm (2–3in) layer of compost at some point before spring. Look after the soil and you shouldn't have to fertilise much, if at all, and water retention will be better, meaning less watering.

+ **Avoid digging to protect soil structure:** because soil is alive, it is best not to dig and turn soil wherever possible, otherwise you disturb your soil's natural processes.

+ **Fast-growing plants may need extra food:** I grow most plants in the ground and these require very little fertiliser if the soil is healthy. Sometimes I give a little boost to plants that grow big and fast in summer and so require lots of nutrients, especially vegetables like tomatoes, courgettes, aubergines and squash, as well as large dahlias and canna. Every two to three weeks in summer I'll apply seaweed or homemade fertilisers, poured on the roots or sprayed on leaves (called a foliar feed). Plants in pots will need more regular fertilising, every week or two in summer. Alternatively, scatter free-range chicken manure pellets every couple of months.

+ **Remove spent flowers to encourage more:** lots of plants can be encouraged to flower more than once (repeat flower) through the summer by cutting off blooms that are starting to look a bit sad, called dead-heading. Most flowers, including those of dahlias, heleniums, salvias, cosmos, roses and zinnias, should be snipped off at the next set of shoots beneath the flower – don't leave the stem. For other plants that grow flower stems from a clump of shoots at ground level (the crown), such as sanguisorbas, astrantias and cirsiums, follow the stem right down and cut near the base, where more will grow. Not all species re-flower.

✛ **Control weeds to prevent them taking over:** reducing weeds in your garden begins with knowing your enemy. Before pulling them up, observe how they grow and spread. This will teach you what the seedlings look like and prevent you from pulling up seedlings of desirable plants. You may even decide you like some weeds and want to keep and control them. Use a hoe or hand hoe to make short work of weed seedlings on hot, dry days, when they can be left on the soil surface to wither. Larger victims can be removed by sliding a hand fork or hori hori vertically down beside the roots to lever them out. Cover large areas with weed-suppressant matting or cardboard to starve them of light over a few months, pinning down with pegs or heavy stones (card is preferable because it decomposes, but ensure it is plain, without print or gloss).

✛ **Prune for better shape and productivity:** pruning isn't actually ever complicated but it is very specific to each plant, making it feel harder than it is. I see crimes against plants every day. People trim shrubs and trees badly, cutting them into round-ish blobs or lopping branches into stumps regardless of the species, which for many will cause irreparable damage. Most shrubs and trees look better when left to grow into their natural shape, and can be contained by thinning the branches rather than chopping them short. I spend time researching each plant online and how it needs to be pruned, then assess the shape before I make a single snip, planning which branch or stems to cut for the best look. Take your time and stand back frequently – thinking time should be longer than cutting time. This way is much better than lopping a branch off quickly only to wish you could stick it back on. Pruning is one of my favourite tasks because there's a real connection between you and the plant. It feels like teamwork.

Tools you'll need

Who knew I could fall so deeply in love with twine? Not I, but it sits firmly in my top three most used tools, sandwiched between secateurs at number one and my trowel. Here I've included a list of my most essential tools and the best ways to use them.

❶ Secateurs: used every single day for dead-heading, pruning and general chopping – they never leave my side.

❷ Natural jute twine: degradable string for tying plants to supports and each other.

❸ Trowel: for planting, weeding and digging small holes.

❹ Hand fork: for wiggling out the intact roots of small weeds.

❺ Hori hori: a sharp Japanese garden knife originally used for wild plant collecting. It is great for dividing plants, digging holes for bulbs and levering out long taprooted weeds, and those growing in cracks in paving.

❻ Hand hoe: for precision weeding around sensitive crops, such as onions and asparagus, and flowering bulbs.

❼ Shears: for neatly trimming hedges and shrubs.

❽ Foldable knife: for preparing cuttings for propagation, harvesting some fruit and vegetables, and quick cutting.

❾ Foldable pruning saw: for cutting 2–4cm (¾in–1⅓in) diameter wooden branches too thick for secateurs. For anything thicker use a larger saw (see below).

❿ Whetstone: for sharpening secateurs and shears after soaking the stone in water for a minute or two.

⓫ Cleaning block: for removing rust and grime from metal gardening tools, like a gritty rubber.

⓬ File: for sharpening larger tools including trowel, hand hoe and spade, and for repairing bigger dents in secateur blades.

Other tools

✛ **Smartphone:** for looking up plants and techniques, and for taking notes.

✛ **Hoe:** for slicing the roots of weeds. Keep it sharp.

✛ **Border spade:** for easy digging and planting.

✛ **Fork:** for lifting larger plants, weeds, potatoes, carrots and other root vegetables.

✛ **Curved hand saw:** for cutting branches up to 10cm (4in) in diameter.

✛ **Mower, hedge cutter and strimmer:** for cutting lawns, brush and hedges. Battery-powered or electric models are more environmentally friendly and quieter than petrol-powered alternatives.

Fill your garden for free!

Learning to propagate your own plants is a fun and rewarding exercise that teaches us how different plants grow. It is a mindful process as you concentrate closely on what you're doing in the moment and then it helps you nurture a personal attachment to the new plant you've grown. It's always a good idea to propagate more plants than you need, because not all of them will flourish.

Environmentally friendly pots and seed trays

Over the last few years I've enjoyed using compostable pots to raise seedlings. These have included peat-free fibre pots made from composted bark and which feel like cardboard. They allow roots to grow through their walls and naturally decompose in the soil (coir is a similar alternative). Using a tool called a soil blocker, you can also make cubes of compacted compost in which to grow seedlings without a pot at all, as roots bind the compost together.

Whether you choose pots or compost blocks, pop them in metal trays or bamboo seed trays to prevent water from dripping everywhere, especially on windowsills and tables inside. For blocks of compost without pots, water gently from the base to prevent them falling apart.

Terracotta pots are useful for growing shrubs and trees from seed or cuttings, when the young plant is likely to stay in the same pot for months or even a couple of years. Bamboo pots work well too. They feel like plastic but after a few years will

Above Alternatives to plastic pots include peat-free fibre, toilet roll tube and bamboo.

degrade as part of a compost heap.

Of course, if you already have plastic pots, keep using them because this saves them from landfill. Some new plastic pots are recyclable, but check with your local recycling plant first. I still prefer to use the alternatives above.

Growing from seed is, on the whole,
straightforward, though some plants
can be harder to raise from seed than
others. Don't be put off when you find
they are. Always follow the instructions
for planting depth and spacing on the
packet. My rule of thumb is to plant the
seed as deep as it is long. For example, a
large pea will be planted 1cm (⅓in) below
the soil surface, while the much smaller
seeds of lettuce will lie just on the
surface or below a dusting of soil.

Any seed that can be sown in the
ground where you ultimately want the
plant to be situated should be – this will
save space indoors. I'll usually sow the
seed for plants that need greater care
and protection, like vegetables, in trays
or pots, which can be kept outside in
a sheltered spot. Here I can continue
growing them, safe from slugs and snails
until the seedlings are large enough to
fend for themselves.

Grow from seed

It doesn't matter how many plants
I grow from seed, seeing the first little
leaves emerging from the compost is
always magical. What's more, I know
the plant hasn't been grown in peat or
treated with inorganic fertilisers and
pesticides, and will be free of disease
because seeds don't carry diseases.

Grow from cuttings

Quick and easy, growing plants from cuttings is one of my favourite activities, and, because it's done at home it's very sustainable. The activity itself I find a mindful one, making me concentrate on what I'm doing and connecting me to the plant as I see it grow, knowing I propagated it. In as little as two to three weeks for many plants, roots start growing and you're on your way to growing a new plant.

Not all plants grow from cuttings but most will, though timing and the part of the plant used can vary. Depending on the plant, cuttings can be taken from new growth that's all green (softwood cuttings), from growth where the top bit is still green and soft but the bottom half has gone woody (semi-ripe cuttings), and from fully woody shoots (hardwood cuttings), suitable for shrubs including roses, buddleia and elder.

Method one: in compost and pots →
I use this method for most cuttings, including rosemary, salvias and *Coleus* (shown).

❶ Between spring and late summer, take a cutting about 10–15cm (4–6in) long from vigorous new growth without flowers. Cut directly beneath one pair of leaves.

❷ Pinch out the growing tip and remove the lower leaves.

❸ Make a hole with your finger or a pencil in a pot of peat-free compost and insert the cutting so the leaves are just above the compost (up to five cuttings per pot), then water. Place in a bright spot out of direct sunlight.

❹ Keep the compost moist while the cuttings root – you may need to cover the cuttings with a transparent lid to keep humidity in, especially indoors.

❺ Once roots show through the holes in the pot and leaves are visibly growing again, gently tease out the cuttings and pot them into individual pots.

Above Persicaria microcephala 'Red Dragon', Coleus and Begonia prior to using them in three different cuttings methods.
Opposite Healthy roots on a cutting of Coleus scutellarioides 'Wedding Train' ready to be planted in a larger pot.

Method two: in water →

I love this method because it's so simple. This works for most plants that root quickly, including dahlia and tomato side shoots, and foliage persicarias (*Persicaria microcephala* 'Red Dragon' shown).

1 Prepare the cutting as for Method one and plonk in a glass of water.
2 Leave in water on a bright windowsill until roots grow to about 5cm (2in).
3 Plant in compost in individual pots.

← Method three: partial leaf cuttings

In the list of mind-boggling things plants can do, growing from leaf cuttings is near the top. Plants that can be propagated like this include *Eucomis*, *Sansevieria* and *Begonia* (shown).

1 Between spring and autumn, cut a new, healthy leaf into strips or squares 2–3cm (about 1in) wide.
2 Lay these pieces flat or poke one cut end a little way into the compost.
3 Water from below, not on the leaves, by dipping the container in water for a few minutes.
4 Place in a bright spot out of direct sun and cover with a lid to keep humid. New shoots will emerge from the cut veins in a few weeks.
5 When new leaves appear, tease out the new plants gently and plant into individual pots of compost.

Other methods to try

✣ **Whole leaf cuttings:** garden succulents such as *Hylotelephium spectabile* and most indoor succulents can be grown from whole leaf cuttings.

Snap a leaf off, leave for a day or two for the cut to dry (callous), then poke that end a little way into compost. Don't cover; succulents prefer drier conditions to prevent rotting.

✣ **Root cuttings:** some plants, including *Echinacea*, *Acanthus* and raspberries, can be grown by cutting off pencil-thick roots in winter while the plant is dormant and burying them horizontally just below the surface in pots of compost left outdoors. In time they'll form a new plant!

✣ **Sticks:** roses, buddleia and elderflower are just three of many shrubs that can be grown from 20cm-long (8in)pieces of woody stem or branch. Cut them from the plant just below buds, forming the base, and cut above buds at the top (this is where roots and shoots grow from). Simply stick the cutting the right way up in the ground or a pot in winter and it should grow in spring.

Three
Encouraging beautiful ecosystems

I've always wanted any garden I design to be a working ecosystem, embodying nature's ability to recycle and renew with low levels of human intervention. If natural ecosystems can be self-sustaining, why not gardens? Nature doesn't need fertiliser or weeding; it keeps going regardless.

A fresh approach to gardening lies in our ability to understand ecology better and think in terms of plant communities rather than isolated elements. Structure, texture and colour should all be considerations, but we should also embrace nature's ability to adapt, change and surprise. There is no end result with ecosystems – their evolution is the constant source of joy.

Turning your space into a beautiful ecosystem is one part letting go of control by having faith that nature will find a balance, and another part making small but intelligent decisions. Don't simply buy a plant because you like the look of it, spend time researching which wildlife will use it, how it spreads and interacts with other plants in the wild, and its suitability to your garden's conditions. Happy plant communities need less maintenance.

What makes a garden ecosystem?

These three elements interact with one another to make up a garden's ecosystem. It's a radical approach to plan a garden in this way, by starting with wildlife and plant interactions, yet it makes total sense for helping the planet and reducing maintenance.

Growing conditions

All ecosystems, wild or in gardens, are defined by the local environment and climate, which dictates which plants will grow well. These conditions include:

+ **Soil:** its type and depth. Is it sand, clay or fine silt? Is it more alkaline or acidic? Does it have lots of organic matter in it, making it fertile, or is it low in nutrients?
+ **Light:** how much direct sunlight does the area receive, and how much of it is in shade?
+ **Water:** how much rainfall is there throughout the year? Are certain seasons dry or wet? Does the ground drain well or does it stay wet?
+ **Exposure:** is the area very windy or sheltered? Does it receive frosts? Is it affected by salt spray from the sea?
+ **Temperature:** what are the maximum and minimum temperatures across the year?

Plant communities

Traditional gardens where everything grows in a set spot can be a little static. In the wild, beauty comes from the dynamism of plants and wildlife that make up an ecosystem mixing over time, creating wonder and surprise.

All ecosystems begin with plants at their core. A naturally occurring group of plants is called a plant community. Plants live alongside one another, competing for space, light, water and nutrients. Everywhere you look in nature you see different plant communities: in a woodland, a pond or meadow, or on a grassy bank, or on scrub land or in the desert. One year a particular species may be dominant, the next another, but all the plants coexist to form a stable community in their chosen habitat.

Such communities can be recreated in gardens by selecting plants that like the same conditions. And here we have an opportunity to be creative, steering the look of our ecosystem to something we enjoy. Our choices can help create an ecosystem that is as dynamic as a wild one but is also something we will enjoy looking at. A successful plant community

Top Hardy grass, *Festuca mairei*, stands out among this complex perennial ecosystem of *Hylotelephium*, *Geranium*, *Origanum* and many other species by designer Piet Oudolf at Scampston Hall in North Yorkshire. **Bottom** Ornamental thistle *Cirsium rivulare* 'Trevor's Blue Wonder' feeding a honey bee, *Apis mellifera*, and common carder bee, *Bombus pascuorum*.

needs little or no watering or fertilising, making it the most sustainable way to grow, and to me, the most satisfying.

Wildlife

Insects primarily, and birds and animals, fertilise flowers to produce seeds and then help spread them. Insects and mammals eat plants, keeping them in check, while fungi and microorganisms in soil break down faeces and plant waste into nutrients for roots to absorb, powering new growth. It's this complex network of interactions that creates an ecosystem.

With your plant community taking shape, it's time to think of the wildlife it might attract and the role it will play as the garden evolves. The aim is to reach a balance where the plants you introduce all coexist harmoniously in a community, while providing food and habitat for wildlife, fungi and more.

How to plan a beautiful ecosystem

One plant is enough to start building an ecosystem; it can be that easy. From there you can add more at your own pace. It's all about observing what's going on in your garden and making adjustments slowly over time.

Think in layers

Across the next few pages I'll take you through the way I plan gardens by planting in layers, starting with static plants that form the building blocks of the garden, working through to weed-suppressing plants and surprise plants that pop up randomly. In the mix are star plants to set the tone and design theme, and spreading plants to encourage the planting to change over time.

While working through each layer of planting, in the back of my mind I always have these overarching core principles:

✛ **Wildlife value:** plants that encourage wildlife
✛ **Seasonality:** planting that changes beautifully with the seasons
✛ **Flux and flow:** planting that shifts and adapts over time
✛ **Framework:** planting that provides structure and a sense of order

The table below shows the way in which each plant layer can contribute to each of the core principles.

		Core principles			
		WILDLIFE VALUE	**SEASONALITY**	**FLUX & FLOW**	**FRAMEWORK**
	Static plants	Yes	Maybe	No	Yes
	Spreading plants	Yes	Maybe	Yes	No
LAYERS OF PLANT BY ROLE	Star plants	Yes	Yes	Maybe	Maybe
	Suppressing plants	Yes	Maybe	Maybe	Maybe
	Surprise plants	Yes	Yes	Yes	No

●	Static plants
●	Spreading plants
●	Star plants
●	Suppressing plants
●	Surprise plants

Above Plan showing layers of planting in the garden on Littlebury Road.

Wildlife value

Usually, the advice to people with small to medium-sized gardens is to grow a limited number of large plants to prevent the space from looking cluttered. 'Less is more,' they say. But I disagree. While this approach does make a space feel neat and appealing, great for a first impression or a photo, in our garden I found it soon became boring, and even less rewarding over time.

Cram plants in for wildlife

Increased diversity of plants provides wildlife with a better range of things to eat, and as with any buffet, more is more. Greater plant diversity will also help to provide suitable habitats for a wider variety of wildlife. In our small garden and on our allotment I have cultivated as many as 400 different species of plant in order to attract the greatest number of wildlife species. The pursuit of variety also keeps my mind actively interested in the garden 365 days of the year.

When making your plant selections, there are two main goals to aim for:

✦ **Maximum diversity:** different insects have evolved to feed off certain shapes of flower, so try to include a mix of different types – daisy-like, spikes, flat-topped – and some plants with big flowers, some with small flowers.
✦ **Indigenous and introduced plants:** many introduced plants from overseas are used by lots of different insects, most of which will forage from a plant no matter where it originated. However, some pickier insects evolved to feed off a smaller number of plants, and sometimes off one single species of plant. By growing a few plants indigenous to your local area among introduced exotics, you will attract and help the largest range of wildlife.

Grow more without feeling cluttered

One of the reasons some people don't like traditional wildlife gardens is because they can look messy, which isn't relaxing. It is true that too many plants and objects, like pots alongside bug hotels, can look busy. In our garden I found the answer is to do more with less using these nifty tricks:

✦ **Strong framework:** include a small number of large plants to give the space instant visual clarity and let the diversity come from the shorter plants around them.

+ **Keep patios and paths simple:** choose paving, gravel or decking that is all one colour and avoid overly fussy patterns. Hard landscaping can act as a minimalist frame to the busier plant picture.
+ **Reduce pots:** try to use only large pots, with multiple plants per pot if necessary. This will also reduce the watering demands of lots of small pots.
+ **Limit colours:** reduce your colour palette to a maximum of three or four main colours, then choose different shades of those colours to instantly create visual order. You can still include a variety of plants while sticking to a limited palette; for instance, *Dahlia* 'Bishop of Canterbury' has bold cerise daisies, as does *Echinacea purpurea* 'Fatal Attraction'. They are different in form but close enough in shape and colour to introduce variety without feeling too cluttered.

Above, left This garden has a good mix of plant species that flower at different times of the year. *Euphorbia characias* subsp. *wulfenii* and *Allium hollandicum* 'Purple Sensation' takes centre stage, underplanted with white *Luzula nivea* in spring. In summer *Verbena hastata* 'Pink Spires', *Salvia* 'Amistad' and *Hydrangea paniculata* 'Little Lime' take over.
Above, right *Eupatorium maculatum* Atropurpureum Group is a magnet for butterflies, including small tortoiseshell, *Aglais urticae*.

Seasonality

I like to exaggerate the passing of time reflected in my garden, but this can only happen with careful plant choices. Get it right and seasonal thinking will benefit wildlife too, by providing year-round shelter and sources of food. It's enjoyable and gives my wellbeing a boost even in the cold dark of winter.

Two gardens in the space of one

Our garden is too small to fit multiple styles of planting; it would be like painting our living room purple on one side and green the other. So when I fell in love with white flowers that didn't match my purple and pink scheme, it was a problem. To get around it I hatched a cunning plan: what if I only planted white flowers for winter and spring, saving pink and purple for summer and autumn? My plan worked and it taught me a really important lesson: not only to work with the seasons, but to learn to grow different plants in the same spaces for beauty at different times of the year. When one plant finishes its main display another takes over in a floral relay race. To take this concept a step further, I try to make entire gardens beautiful in all seasons, offering something for both wildlife and us every month.

Think seasonally

I won't lie, it is tricky to strike the balance, and our white spring garden never quite looks as full as the summer garden. Each year I keep trying and it tiptoes a bit closer. In one corner I have snowdrops, white hellebores and white daffodils (*Narcissus* 'Thalia'), providing bright white flowers through winter to be enjoyed by active bumblebees. As the weather warms in spring, *Geranium* 'Anne Thomson' emerges in the same spot to hide the dying bulb foliage, and *Dahlia* 'Bishop of Canterbury' bursts over this in summer. The hellebores and geranium cope with some shade from the dahlia. Another corner has deciduous shrubs *Buddleia davidii* 'Santana' and *Sambucus nigra* f. *porphyrophylla* 'Black Lace' with spring bulbs beneath them. The bulbs make the most of the light before the new buddleia leaves emerge and *Clematis viticella* 'Galore Evipo032' grows through it, flowering before and after the buddleia for triple the flowers in summer and autumn.

I always think beyond flowers when planning seasonally: foliage impact is more important because it is present for longer and with greater mass. *Schefflera rhododendrifolia* with its compound palmate leaves and *Begonia palmata* 'Tie Dye's leaves are striking year-round.

Top Drifts of snowdrops, *Galanthus nivalis*, flower in late winter under deciduous shrubs before their leaves emerge.
Bottom *Buddleia davidii* 'Santana' is a vibrant summer shrub that can tolerate small climbers growing through it, such as *Clematis viticella* 'Polish Spirit'.

Stems, branches, dying plants and seed heads that hold their shape are often overlooked but offer a different kind of beauty in winter.

Here I've listed the visual characteristics of plants through different seasons and how they can benefit wildlife in your garden through the year:

+ **Flowers for colour:** nectar and pollen are eaten by insects
+ **Seedheads for structure:** seeds are eaten by birds and mice
+ **Berries for decoration:** eaten by birds and mammals
+ **Dried stems for shape:** shelter for insects in winter
+ **Tree trunks for sculpture:** shelter for birds, squirrels, insects and snails
+ **Ornamental grass leaves:** food for caterpillars when green, shelter when dry and brown
+ **Leaf litter:** shelter for frogs, toads and hedgehogs, food for worms and insects

The strong path line frames the airy planting in this tricky part-shade area, featuring Hydrangea 'Limelight', Calamagrostis brachytricha, Anemone hupehensis var. japonica 'September Charm' and Geranium 'Anne Thomson'.

Framework

There is a fine line between 'natural look' ecosystems and a tatty, chaotic scrappy patch. You can stay on the right side of that line by establishing a good framework for your garden. This will hold everything else together and offer a pleasing sense of order.

Using a framework

In nature plants don't necessarily have a fixed position. They spread, and the feeling of randomness, of plants moving and mingling, is part of the appeal. I like to recreate this effect in gardens but in a way that looks deliberate, not messy, using structural plants and the edges of hard landscaping, lawns or vertical structures to hold a scene together. Here are some different frameworks that you can put into practice in your garden.

+ **Outlines:** whether it's the edge of a neat lawn, a patio or path, straight or curved, it brings visual sense to what can otherwise be a complex and confusing picture. If you don't like a hard edge, don't worry, plants will naturally grow over parts of it to soften the effect. In the vertical plane, trees and shrubs can frame planting, as do walls, doors and arches.

+ **Backdrops:** a wall, fence or neatly trimmed hedge can help the plants' shape and texture to stand out. Think about the colour and finish of the backdrop to prevent planting from blending in with it too much.

+ **Structural plants:** one of the fastest and best ways of adding a framework to the garden is to include plants that hold a bold shape through most of the year. The shape can be anything you choose, from spire-shaped trees or rounded shrubs to vertical grasses or cacti. Even if everything else around it has been flattened by wind, the area can still look good if it contains a number of these structural plants.

+ **Patchworks:** a mix of shapes and textures is more important than colour. Aim for a mixture of fluffy plants to glue everything together (e.g. fountain-shaped grass *Sporobolus heterolepis*), vertical plants as accents (e.g. *Veronicastrum virginicum*) and horizontal plants to create a breathing space (*Hylotelephium spectabile*).

+ **Randomised repetition:** avoid planting in obvious lines and instead dot plants around your garden. I plant in odd-numbered groups of three, five, etc., spaced roughly equally, but not quite. This technique creates balance and order while gently masking the artifice, thanks to a touch of imperfection.

Flux and flow

Natural landscapes are in a constant state of flux. Plants spread and seed around, flowing back and forth as they compete for space, a slow green tide advancing and receding over time. In the wild, shrubs grow, trees fall, flowers appear in their wake. No garden stays the same, but in my garden (and later designs) I opened the door for nature to work its wild magic by planning areas for plants to spread into naturally.

Moving plants

I first noticed that our plants were moving when *Monarda* 'Cambridge Scarlet' kept sending its rhizomes northwards along our raised bed. Each year it moved 30cm (12in) to the left of its original position, clearly preferring the conditions away from where I'd planted it. *Nicotiana knightiana* didn't seem to want to stay put either; its seeds have gradually migrated into shadier spots where it's happier. I enjoyed the idea that each year the plants themselves would adapt to their conditions and change how the garden looked ever so slightly.

Despite the planting being tropical, our garden was starting to behave like a meadow, where plants naturally flowed into new areas as their populations fluctuated in size. I had a niggling feeling that to completely relinquish control could lead to chaos, so I put in place a few strategies to guide these natural processes.

Above Self-sowers: spires of *Lysimachia atropurpurea* 'Beaujolais', globes of *Allium cristophii*, orange *Calendula officinalis* and white *Nigella damascena* 'Green Pod'.

Ratios

Our garden has a ratio of spreading to static plants of about 30:70. In gardens I've designed for other people, where low maintenance is more important, I aim for a ratio of 20:80, which still allows for some flow of plants. Experiment to find the right balance for you.

Above Monarda didyma is particularly useful because it slowly sends out rhizomes into new areas without taking over.

Guiding a state of flux

First, I mentally split our plants into two camps: those I knew would be static and stay put (see p.62) and plants I suspected to be spreading by rhizome, runner or seeds (see p.67). By installing a framework of patio and paths as well as static plants, mostly consisting of chunky shrubs, I could limit the ground into which the spreaders could move.

It became useful to learn exactly how and when the plants spread. This allowed me to recognise new seedlings and shoots, then make a decision as to which should stay or go, thinning out excess numbers.

To begin with I was worried this largely hands-off approach could lead to a chaotic garden, but that wasn't the case at all. The plants moved to where they naturally wanted to grow, grew more healthily, and interlocked like a puzzle, filling gaps tightly to limit each other's spread and prevent unwanted plants from gaining a foothold.

Observing the flux and flow of plants became a mindful activity that I enjoyed dipping into now and again. I never quite knew what was going to happen. Guiding it was pretty easy because, let's face it, these are plants we're talking about – even snails move a thousand times faster. But I also felt profoundly reassured knowing I wasn't in control of what happened, I wasn't totally responsible. It was a partnership with the plants.

There's a certain kind of beauty found only in serendipity. In gardens it is only made possible by growing things in a constant state of flux.

Star plants

Star plants are those you really love and want to stand out more than others, setting the tone and style of your space. Any plant can be a star, be it a perennial, annual, climber, shrub or tree. The defining factor is that it's a star in your eyes.

Left Self-sown rusty foxglove *Digitalis ferruginea* 'Gigantea' draws the eye because of its shape, in front of *Kniphofia* 'Tawny King' and grass *Nassella tenuissima*.

know that everything around them will need to coordinate with those tall white spires of flower, allowing you to plan accordingly.

Constellations of plants

I deliberately choose a number of star plants that differ in shape, creating a mix that is interesting in itself even before factoring in colour. In our garden the star plants in summer are dahlias with chunky flowers, loose and airy salvias and persicarias for strong vertical spires. I repeat the combination in spots around the garden for a larger constellation of star plants, which adds to the overall garden framework.

It's fun to play with different combinations of plant shapes. Sometimes I use star plants that are all different shapes, at other times plants that are all similar in form. For instance, by choosing only tall, upright flowers, such as *Veronicastrum* and *Kniphofia*, you can achieve a striking otherworldly look.

Setting your garden's style

I tend to have one or two star plants in mind before I even start planning a planting area. They are a starting point for deciding the colours and textures to use throughout the garden.

For instance, if your star plants have big leaves, your garden's style will swing towards tropical, whereas grasses and large, bright daisies suggest meadows or prairies. If you love white foxgloves, you

Left A mix of *Allium giganteum* and *A. hollandicum* 'Purple Sensation', star plants of late spring, underplanted with *Erysimum* 'Bowles Mauve'.

Different stars in different seasons

All plants have a main season or two when they visually stand out more than at other times, usually because of their flowers, though it can also be the foliage that makes an impact. In autumn in our garden, the standout dark purple foliage of annual *Ricinus communis* 'New Zealand Black' becomes a star. In other gardens I've planted, *Cotinus coggygria* 'Flame', with bright red autumnal foliage, becomes the focal point.

More than any other plant, think about what your star plants will do throughout the year. You're likely to need a different set for different seasons. Tulips and alliums flower from spring to early summer before passing the baton to echinaceas in mid-summer and then rudbeckias.

Some plants with particularly long flowering periods, like salvias, can be a star plant across as many as three seasons, allowing you to partner them with a number of other star plants that are around for a shorter time, such as alliums in late spring, agapanthus in mid-summer and nerines in autumn.

Star plants I've trialled in gardens

Perennial

- *Canna* spp. – for a tropical effect, I use 'Assaut' and 'Shenandoah' for purple leaves, 'Durban' for electric-orange variegation and the tall 'Bird of Paradise'.
- *Cirsium rivulare* – a wonderful thistle that repeat flowers, 'Atropurpureum' is crimson-pink but my favourite is 'Trevor's Blue Wonder', curiously magenta.
- *Dahlia* spp. – I enjoy growing it from seed and it is loved by pollinators. 'Bishop of Canterbury' has rich magenta single flowers and *D. merckii* is a species with pale purple flowers.
- *Daucus carota* – like *Ammi* and *Anthriscus*, airy white flat-topped lacy flowers in summer, here with strong winter structure.
- *Digitalis ferruginea* 'Gigantea' – a short-lived perennial with tall spikes of rusty flowers, will self-seed like *D. purpurea*.
- *Echinacea* – *E. pallida* is a strong species with pale pink petals drooping down from the large daisy flowers, with bold seed heads in winter loved by birds.
- *Echinops ritro* – globe thistles that seem to float over planting, 'Veitch's Blue' and white 'Arctic Glow'.
- *Helenium* – 'Waltraut' and 'Sahin's Early Flowering' I've found strong and reliable.
- *Persicaria amplexicaulis* – bulletproof plants with masses of narrow, upright spires of flowers. 'September Spires' has long pink spires, 'White Eastfield' white flowers with gold calyxes, and 'Ample Pink' an abundance of waist-high flowers.
- *Rudbeckia fulgida* var. *deamii* – has rich yellow daisies from summer to autumn.
- *Salvia* spp. – shrubs in all manner of shapes and colours, perfect for summer flower power. Reliable varieties: 'Amistad', 'Amante', 'Nachtvlinder', 'Cerro Potosí', 'California Sunset', 'Clotted Cream'.
- *Symphyotrichum* spp. – asters come in shades of white, pale blue on the short 'Little Carlow', through to dark purple of tall 'Violetta'. Essential for late summer colour.
- *Verbena bonariensis* – used a lot by garden designers for good reason, a gentle self-sower with very tall stems with purple flowers.
- *Verbena hastata* – masses of spikes of flower in different colours, 'Pink Spires', 'White Spires'.
- *Veronicastrum virginicum* – beautiful whorls of leaves up robust stems leading to a spike of white flowers on 'Album'.

Top A sea of tulips in designer Charles Rutherfoord and Rupert Tyler's garden.
Bottom *Helenium* 'Waltraut'.

Annual/biennial

- *Ammi majus/A. visnaga* – airy, white lacy flowers all summer long; I love 'Green Lace'.
- *Anthriscus sylvestris* – similar airy white flowers in early summer.
- *Cosmos bipinnatus* – airy foliage with flowers all summer; 'Antiquity' is faded magenta and 'Purity' white.
- *Nicotiana alata* – 'Lime Green' has bright, acid-green flowers through summer with evening scent.
- *Zinnia elegans* – very solid daisy flowers, 'Queen Lime' is a zingy green and 'Queen Lime Red' a mix of green and terracotta.

Bulbs

- *Agapanthus* spp. – late summer flowers. I love white cultivars most, such as 'Snow Cloud', though also blue 'Northern Star'.
- *Allium* spp. – there are many alliums for different seasons, but my stars are the late spring giants 'Purple Sensation', 'Giganteum' and 'Mount Everest', as well as the summer-flowering *A. sphaerocephalon*.
- *Narcissus* spp. – my favourite daffodils are white 'Thalia', yellow wild daffodil *N. pseudonarcissus* and the pale yellow *N. bulbocodium* 'Arctic Bells'.
- *Nerine* spp. – an autumn-flowering bulb, *N. bowdenii* is widely regarded as the hardiest species and beautiful, though there are many cultivars in different colours.
- *Tulipa* spp. – I aim to only plant tulips I know to reliably flower every year, since so many cultivars fizzle out after the first. I grow the Viridiflora types, such as 'Green Star', and species tulips, such as *T. turkestanica* and *T. humilis* 'Little Beauty'.

Top Dahlia 'Thomas A. Edison'.
Middle Cosmos bipinnatus 'Cupcakes White', Ammi visnaga 'Green Mist' and Persicaria amplexicaulis 'Firetail'.
Bottom Zinnia elegans 'Queen Lime Red'.

Static plants

Static plants don't spread or multiply. They stay put, guarding their spot, blocking unwanted plants or excess spreaders from growing there. This makes them essential for reducing the day-to-day effort needed to look after your garden's ecosystem.

Growing a framework

Because they have real presence and structure, static plants form the essential framework of your garden. Owing to their important role, you may want to start planning your ecosystem by positioning static plants first. They may grow larger over time, but are reliable enough to plant in the ground and then be left alone.

In our garden we grow evergreen *Brahea armata, Cordyline australis, Schefflera taiwaniana, Fatsia polycarpa* 'Green Fingers' and deciduous *Sambucus nigra* f. *porphyrophylla* 'Black Lace'. Most sit around the perimeter of the garden, forming a lush boundary to contain the spreaders (see p.67). Hedges are the prime example of a static plant as a structured backdrop, ever present and easy to look after. Our surrounding shrubs are essentially an informal hedge.

Static plants don't always have to be substantial. We do have some smaller static plants that are tough enough not to be smothered by others, such as the fern *Polystichum setiferum* and a number of *Aeonium arboreum* 'Zwartkop' dotted around.

If you find the maintenance of your garden is getting too much, add more static plants; the more you have, the less maintenance your garden's ecosystem will need. Be careful, though: too many static plants and the space becomes less interesting.

Below Spiky *Cordyline australis* and glaucous blue of a pollarded *Eucalyptus gunnii* form a static and evergreen backbone to the exuberant planting in Littlebury Road.

A home for wildlife

Generally static plants are bigger, permanent plants: shrubs, large perennials, big ornamental grasses, hedges and trees. Their large roots and stems are excellent for locking in carbon, and simultaneously form the basis of safe habitats for birds, mammals and insects.

Thanks to their permanence, static plants can be relied upon to provide both shelter and sustenance for wildlife over many seasons. Grasses are used by insects to hide and hibernate over winter, while larger shrubs and trees give birds places to roost and nest. With the right plant selections you can increase the garden's use to wildlife. Choose winter-flowering plants such as hellebores for winter-active and early-emerging bumblebees and those that produce berries and fruit in autumn for birds, such as *Crataegus monogyna*. Static plants have the greatest mass in your ecosystem and therefore the most to offer wildlife in your area.

Top Palms like this beautiful silver *Brahea armata* are excellent static plants. Their wildlife benefit comes from providing shelter for insects and birds in winter.
Bottom Hawthorn, *Crataegus monogyna*, is an excellent and beautiful small tree that can also be cut as a hedge or shrub.

Static plants I've trialled in gardens

Small trees

- *Cornus kousa* var. *chinensis* – early summer flowers, autumn fruit for birds if you have multiple trees; 'White Fountain' and 'Milky Way' are beautiful.
- *Hoheria sexstylosa* – a rarely seen evergreen with summer flowers for insects; try 'Stardust'.
- *Malus sylvestris* (crab apple) – spring blossom and autumn fruit for wildlife.
- *Pinus sylvestris* 'Watereri'– a small cultivar of this larger tree with dense evergreen foliage for nesting birds.
- *Pittosporum tenuifolium* – I like 'Variegatum' and 'Purpureum', with whorls of leaves, offering good shelter for birds.

Medium trees

- *Betula utilis* var. *jacquemontii* – good for wildlife and large without creating too much shade (grows to a height of approx. 10m/33ft).

Exotic

- *Brahea armata* – evergreen structure provides shelter for insects in winter.
- *Ensete ventricosum* 'Maurelii' is a non-hardy banana alternative; bring inside in winter.
- *Musa sikkimensis* (banana) – a hardy plant, 'Red Tiger' has striped young leaves.
- *Phormium* spp. – insects hibernate among its tightly packed leaves.

Shrubs and hedges

- *Baptisia australis* – dusky blue-purple spires of flower, plus a white variety.
- *Eucalyptus pulverulenta* – a dwarf gum tree with beautiful structure, sold as 'Baby Blue'. Or *E. gunnii* can be pollarded as a shrub.
- *Euphorbia characias* subsp. *wulfenii* – acid-green flowers in early summer.
- *Fuchsia magellanica* – the white 'Hawkshead' is beautiful in shade.
- *Hydrangea* spp. – in a range of colours and sizes; *H. paniculata* 'Little Lime' grows to 1m (3ft), large *H. aspera* Villosa Group has flat flowers in violet, as does *H. macrophylla* 'Blue Wave' (pink on alkaline soil).
- *Mahonia* spp. – my favourites are *M. eurybracteata* subsp. *ganpinensis* 'Soft Caress' and *M. oiwakensis*.
- *Melianthus major* – remarkable glaucous-silver leaves with saw-toothed edges.
- *Pinus wallichiana* 'Nana' and *P. mugo* – there are many quirky dwarf conifers worth considering, but these two are very reliable.
- *Sambucus nigra* – 'Black Lace' has finely dissected leaves and pink flowers.
- *Taxus baccata* – as hedges or clipped topiary shapes.

Top Betula utilis var. jacquemontii.
Middle Ensete ventricosum 'Maurelii' surrounded by Dahlia 'Pink Giraffe'.
Bottom Hydrangea macrophylla 'Blue Wave'; growing in alkaline soil turns the flowers pink.

Grasses

- *Calamagrostis* x *acutiflora* 'Karl Foerster' – strong upright form.
- *Carex grayii* – remarkable small plant with mace-shaped seed heads.
- *Jarava ichu* – waist-high airy white seedheads.
- *Miscanthus giganteus* – 3-m (10ft) tall deciduous grass.
- *Miscanthus sinensis* 'Morning Light' – vase-shaped chest-high grass.
- *Molinia caerulea* subsp. *arundinacea* 'Transparent' – low mounded leaves with tall seedheads that are easily seen through.
- *Panicum virgatum* 'Northwind' – strong vertical shape with fluffy seedheads.

Perennial

- *Dryopteris wallichiana* – large upright fern.
- *Kniphofia* spp. – large 'Tawny King', 'Green Jade', small 'Mango Popsicle' and 'Lemon Popsicle'.
- *Phlomis russeliana* – towers of yellow whorled flowers.
- *Polystichum setiferum* – large fountain-shaped fern.

Climbers

- *Clematis viticella* 'Polish Spirit', 'Little Nell', 'Galore Evipoo32' – small to medium climber flowering all summer.
- *Hedera helix* 'Glacier' – white-edged ivy for lightening shady spots.
- *Parthenocissus henryana* – a smaller Boston ivy with variegated purple tinted leaves.
- *Passiflora caerulea* 'White Lightning' – vigorous passion flower with white flowers.
- *Rosa* 'Iceberg', 'Gertrude Jekyll' – reliable climbing roses.
- *Schizophragma hydrangeoides* var. *concolor* 'Moonlight' – a remarkable climbing hydrangea with silvery leaves.
- *Trachelospermum jasminoides* – evergreen jasmine with beautiful scent.

Top Calamagrostis brachytricha.
Middle Carex grayii.
Bottom Kniphofia 'Tawny King'.
Left Dryopteris wallichiana and Hydrangea 'Little Lime'.

Deschampsia cespitosa 'Pixie Fountain' spreads around gently by seed.

Spreading plants

Spreading plants are the rebels, able to reproduce easily by seed or by sending out shoots. Each year you can either let them fight it out among themselves, or lend a helping hand by pulling some out.

Good for planet and pocket

What I love about spreading plants is that they reproduce for free, especially when you've matched a plant with its favourite growing conditions. Suddenly you have an unlimited supply of plants that haven't been transported anywhere, watered, fertilised or raised in plastic pots.

I only grow my absolute favourite spreaders, and I also try to make sure they are good for wildlife; you don't want these prolific plants detracting from your ecosystem-building efforts.

Observing and controlling spreading plants

Monitor your spreading plants carefully: every plant spreads at different rates in different conditions, and no two gardens are the same. Give any plant at least a couple of seasons. The amount one plant can spread can induce panic at first, but it may turn out to be easy to pull out or hoe, or the seedlings may be eaten in volume by slugs and snails. On the face of it, spreaders that multiply by runner or rhizome can be easier to control because you can see where they are growing, though they also form strong root systems that can keep coming back.

✢ **Self-sown seeds (e.g. *Eryngium giganteum* and *Echinacea pallida*):** seeds are spread around the parent by various means and to various distances depending on the plant. Learn to recognise seedlings early on to make it easy to pull them out or hoe them. Cut off the seed heads of prolific self-seeders before they start turning brown and ripen, to reduce numbers of seedlings.

✢ **Stolons (e.g. strawberries):** horizontal shoots above ground form new plants away from the parent wherever the shoot touches and roots into the soil. Keep an eye out for the runners forming and cut them off to reduce their spread or reduce the overall plant by as much as a half. Burn, bin or bury these at the bottom of the compost bin, otherwise they may grow in the compost!

✢ **Rhizomes (e.g. *Monarda didyma* and *Pennisetum macrourum*):** horizontal roots underground send up new shoots a short distance from the parent plant. Dig out unwanted new plants.

Spreading plants I've trialled

Seeding plants
- *Calendula* spp. – I like 'Snow Princess', 'Touch of Red' and 'Sunset Buff'.
- *Centaurea nigra* – bright purple small thistle flowers all summer.
- *Deschampsia cespitosa* – a mound-forming grass, short-lived but easy to move seedlings around.
- *Digitalis purpurea* – biennial with pink or white spires of flower.
- *Eryngium giganteum* – a biennial with silver spiky flowers.
- *Hylotelephium* spp. – perennial 'Purple Emperor' and 'Jose Aubergine'.
- *Knautia arvensis* – perennial with pale blue-pink flowers held high.
- *Knautia macedonica* – waist-high perennial with burgundy flowers.
- *Luzula nivea* – small, white-flowered grass-like woodland plant for shade.
- *Nicotiana knightiana* and *N. langsdorfii* – annual.
- *Nigella damascena* 'Green Pod' – annual.
- *Papaver somniferum* – annual, well-drained soil.
- *Persicaria orientalis* –annual.
- *Tellima grandiflora* – perennial.

Temporary filler plants
In any newly planted area there will be bare areas of soil while everything else grows to full size, which can take a year or two. To fill those gaps temporarily I choose annuals that I know won't shade everything else too much and will eventually die when the main plants crowd them out. Many annual surprise plants (p.72) are perfect for this, and I also use:

- *Ammi* spp.
- *Calendula* spp.
- *Cosmos bipinnatus*
- *Erysimum* spp. (wallflower)
- *Nigella damascena*
- *Silene dioica*
- *Tropaeolum majus* or *T. minus* (nasturtium)

Top Eschscholzia californica.
Bottom Persicaria orientalis.

Runner- and rhizome-forming plants

- *Achillea millefolium* – the species, with white or pink flowers, is lovely; 'Terracotta' has fantastic orange colour.
- *Anemone* x *hybrida* – 'Honorine Jobert' in white and 'Pamina' in pink.
- *Araiostegia hymenophylloides* – fantastic fine-leaved spreading fern. Perennial.
- *Euphorbia amygdaloides* – spreading woodland plant with acid-green spring flowers. Perennial, part shade.
- *Monarda didyma* – colourful and unusual flowerheads, will gently spread. I use 'Cambridge Scarlet' and the pink 'On Parade'.
- *Tiarella cordifolia* – perennial.
- *Vinca minor* – a low-growing spreader, *alba* with white flowers and 'Atropurpurea' for purple.

Top Lysimachia atropurpurea 'Beaujolais', Digitalis purpurea and Nigella damascena 'Green Pod'.
Middle, left Achillea millefolium 'Cerise Queen'.
Middle, right Anemone x hybrida 'Honorine Jobert'.
Bottom Calendula officinalis 'Snow Princess'.

Suppressing plants

Any plant that grows so densely it completely covers the ground, blocking sunlight and making it hard for seedlings to grow beneath, is a suppressing plant. If your garden is hard to look after and needs weeding constantly, it's time to make better use of your suppressing plant layer.

Blanketing plants

The suppressors can be large, static plants with dense foliage, like most hedging or evergreen shrubs. When planning a garden, however, I think of them more as low-growing plants that usually spread outwards, also called ground-cover plants. They do cross over with the spreading plant layer – many plants will tick both boxes – but the key distinction is that suppressors must grow densely enough to reduce other growth.

These plants will cover bare soil where unwanted plants grow, reducing the amount of maintenance your garden needs. This looks better too, as you have no wasted space, and it protects soil from water runoff. And, of course, more plant volume and cover is good for wildlife, providing shelter and food.

Functional yet fabulous

Although suppressing plants are included in the garden for functionality, I still select them for their appearance. Because they are usually quite low and spreading, forming a dense carpet, I treat them just as you would an indoor

Above *Epimedium grandiflorum.*

carpet, choosing plants that match the overall style of the garden and its colour scheme, usually thinking of them as a backdrop to everything else.

Suppressing plants I've trialled

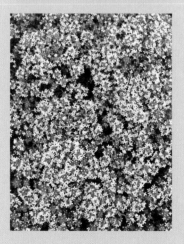

Naturally spreading

- *Adiantum venustum* – evergreen maidenhair fern for shade.
- *Asarum europaeum* – glossy rounded leaves forming a low carpet in shade.
- *Epimedium grandiflorum* – ethereal spring flowers over tough suppressing leaves.
- *Euphorbia amygdaloides* var. *robbiae* – vigorous woodland plant for part shade including dry soils.
- *Geranium* x *oxonianum* – small with pale pink flowers in part shade.
- *Geranium psilostemon* – large with bright magenta flowers in full shade.
- *Pachysandra terminalis* – whorls of shiny leaves in full shade.
- *Stachys byzantina* – velvety leaves used by wool carder bees (*Anthidium manicatum*).
- *Thymus serpyllum* – creeping thyme forms a low blanket with flowers in late spring.
- *Tradescantia pallida* – not fully hardy, will create a dense spreading carpet of purple.
- *Vinca major* – lilac-blue flowers, or white on 'Alba'.
- *Viola odorata* – part-shade-loving carpet-forming spring flower in blue, purple or white.

Clump-forming (to grow in groups)

- *Astrantia major* – full sun to part-shade.
- *Brunnera macrophylla* 'Mr Morse' – part-shade.
- *Heuchera* – suitable for sun or shade depending on the cultivar. 'Licorice' has shiny dark-purple leaves, 'Marmalade' ginger with red undersides, 'Paris' and 'Isabella' repeat pink flowers all summer, 'Thomas' tall white flowers, and 'Green Tea' is a small pink-flowering variety.

Top Astrantia major subsp. involucrata 'Shaggy' and Nassella tenuissima.
Middle Euphorbia amygdaloides var. robbiae.
Bottom Thymus serpyllum 'Snowdrift'.

Surprise plants

In a further attempt to bring untamed nature to our door, I like to introduce an element of serendipity to gardens, using surprise plants. These are gentle self-seeders or spreaders that I add knowing they will pop up when or where I least expect it, brightening my day.

Plan for surprises

Once, tired after a long day of walking up and down hillside meadows, I felt a butterfly flutter past my face. Following its gentle arc I watched it land on a tiny silver spire, glowing in the short grass: autumn lady's tresses, the wild orchid *Spiranthes spiralis*. I wish I could bottle my feelings at stumbling across this beautiful wildflower.

Surprise is a key ingredient of nature's exquisite beauty. At times when I make such a discovery I feel really alive, hyper-aware of the natural connections all around me that have evolved over millions of years. It's that feeling that I want to evoke both in my garden designs and when I'm gardening.

Qualities of a surprise plant

Surprise plants fall into two groups: those with a short flowering period and dormant for most of the year, and those that seed around randomly. Both pop up to flower before we notice they're there, growing flower stems rapidly to catch us off guard.

Another trait of surprise plants is that they are able to grow well in crowded planting areas or out of tiny cracks in patios and walls. This allows them to grow among our other plants without us noticing, before firing up those quick-growing surprise flowers.

Uninvited guests

Of course, the best surprises come from those plants we didn't choose, their seeds germinating after years in the soil, blown in on the wind or deposited in bird droppings. Every now and then one of these perceived weeds will grow into something spectacular.

One year a pure white petunia grew unexpectedly in one of our window boxes. I don't much like petunias but this one I left, admiring its existence against the odds. I have to say, it was one of the prettiest and most vigorous plants I grew that year.

Every now and then it's worth keeping an unrecognised seedling until you know what it is – it may be your next star plant.

Surprise plants I've trialled

- *Anemone coronaria* (Saint Bridgid Group) 'The Admiral' – bright flowers grow from corms (like bulbs) in spring and autumn. has bright pink flowers.
- *Anemone nemorosa* – spring flowers from corms in shades of white and blue.
- *Antirrhinum majus* – self-sowing annuals in various colours.
- *Centaurea cyanus* – cornflowers that self-sow in bare soil in white, pink and blue. 'Black Ball' is a near-black purple.
- *Crocus* spp. – spring flowers from bulbs that pop up in lawns and among other low-growing plants.
- *Digitalis* spp. (foxgloves) – self-sowing biennials with tall pink or white flower spires that can pop up among other plants.
- *Fritillaria meleagris* – beautiful chequered purple or white flowers spring out of low plants, meadows and lawns.
- *Galanthus nivalis* (snowdrops) – bright white bulbs to surprise you in the dark of winter.
- *Geranium* 'Ann Folkard' – acts like a mini-climber, scrambling loosely through other plants, its bright magenta flowers popping out from behind others.
- *Linaria purpurea* – self-sowing here and there, its purple flowers popping up through others.
- *Papaver cambricum* – yellow, orange or red Welsh poppy that grows well in shade, bringing surprise pops of colour where you least expect it.
- *Papaver orientale* – this poppy is perennial, coming back in the same spot, but its fleeting moment always surprises.
- *Papaver somniferum* – one of the most beautiful self-sowing poppies, in varying shades of pale-pink to dark purple. Its large seed heads are great for drying.
- *Verbena bonariensis* – self-sows among other plants, popping out above them!

Top Crocus vernus 'Pickwick'.
Middle Anemone coronaria (Saint Bridgid Group) 'The Admiral'.
Bottom Papaver orientale 'Princess Victoria Louise'.

Erupting planting areas

It's often our tendency to want to tame plants and keep them under control, but I'd like to encourage everyone to let them run rampant, at least a little. Include some areas in your garden that burgeon with beauty, as though the plants are exploding out of the ground with increased drama and energy.

Overflowing with plants

In some areas of the gardens I design, I actively encourage groups of plants that almost look like an eruption of flowers or foliage, as though someone has set off fireworks and paused the aftermath.

Generally these plants have vertical upright stems or an arching fountain shape, but crucially the stems must be tall and narrow, so that you are able to see through them. A few of these dotted among shorter plants will burst out dramatically.

Rather than planting them all at the back of the border, I scatter them around, including in the front of a planting, near paths and patios, in spots where I know they won't get in the way. It's nice brushing your arms and hands against them in summer.

Left I love walking along this path, it's like swimming through plants: Cleome hassleriana 'Violet Queen', Cyperus involucratus, Persicaria amplexicaulis 'September Spires', Dahlia 'Thomas A. Edison', Verbena bonariensis and Echium pininana 'Pink Fountain'.

Explosive effect plants I've trialled

- *Calamagrostis brachytricha* –
  a large fountain-shaped grass
  with fluffy seed heads.
- *Cephalaria gigantea* – giant
  scabious with beautiful leaves
  and large yellow-green flowers
  at head height.
- *Pennisetum* 'Fairy Tales' –
  fountain-shaped leaves with
  long seed heads like rockets.
- *Persicaria amplexicaulis*
  'September Spires' – a mound
  of flowers with long pink
  flower spires held on long
  stems.
- *Salvia* 'Amante' and 'Amistad'
  – shrubs that grow outwards
  into a vase shape with firework
  flowers in purple and rich
  cerise.
- *Sanguisorba officinalis* 'Red
  Thunder' – small mounds of
  attractive leaves fire up tall,
  wiry stems with bobbles of
  dark red flower.
- *Sanguisorba tenuifolia* var. *alba*
  – finely cut leaves sit below
  head-height wiry stems with
  white flower heads all summer
  (may need supports).
- *Stipa gigantea* – a clump-
  forming grass sending up wiry
  head-height seed heads.

Clockwise, from top left
Sanguisorba officinalis 'Red
Thunder'; S. officinalis 'Martin's
Mulberry' flows over purple artichoke
'Violet de Provence'; spires of Salvia
nemorosa 'Caradonna' burst out of the
raised bed with those of Lysimachia
atropurpurea 'Beaujolais'; Perovskia
'Blue Spire' and Calamagrostis
brachytricha both have an explosive
form.

Finding beauty in imperfection

As the seasons rolled past in our garden I came to worry less about insect damage to leaves. In fact, I started to enjoy seeing these little indicators of life. Now I stop to wonder, why did we ever start caring about nibbled leaves when the very thing we love about nature is its imperfection?

Damage, death and decay

There was a time when I would snip off nibbled leaves and remove all dead flowers, tidying the garden. Then, I started to see the beauty in the seed heads of some flowers like *Allium cristophii* and *Dipsacus fullonum*, leaving them on the plants. A dead tree too, with its barkless trunk, bone white among tawny grasses in autumn, made a natural sculpture.

I fell in love with this final part of the plant life cycle, known as senescence, the slow decline towards death. When the plant then moves beyond into decay, it completes the cycle as bacteria, fungi and soil organisms decompose it into nutrients used by seedlings that will form the next generation.

I find acknowledging this process comforting and reassuring, helping me connect better to the natural cycle of life, death and renewal. Even the smell of leaf litter decomposing slowly creates a timeless woodland memory.

Of course, wildlife needs this process too. Clear away all dead plant material and we cut out an important piece of our garden ecosystem.

Wonderful wonkiness

I've always preferred imperfection in art and design, and asymmetric shapes feel more welcoming to me than formal symmetry. Perhaps it is because I, like everyone, am imperfect.

In the wild, few trees grow bolt upright; instead they lean slightly in the wind or grow with an asymmetrical shape caused by damage inflicted when younger. In gardens, trees and shrubs can be grown in this more natural way too; it contributes to making a space feel wild and natural, and again makes a garden more relaxed. You don't always have to worry about keeping trunks completely straight.

If a plant grows too large and flops over a path, we can prop it up or we can leave it to soften the landscape and brush our ankles, a sensation we would otherwise miss. The plant can be cut back later, at the end of winter. If something is in the way by all means deal with it, but ask yourself if you are being overly tidy.

Opposite *Asplenium scolopendrium* and *Hosta fortunei* 'Francee' are lush shade-loving plants, making them susceptible to the odd nibble from snails and caterpillars, but this doesn't affect their overall look.

Winter structure and appreciation

When planning a garden for all seasons (see p.52), one exciting element to consider is its structure in winter. This can make an outdoor space look good even in the dullest months, and can come from a variety of elements: patios, paths, evergreen plants, tree trunks and, less often discussed, dead plants.

Structure from dead plants

Annuals and many perennials die back to ground level in winter, but some will hold their structure thanks to strong stems and shapely seed heads. When everything in the garden has died back, muted by duller days and fewer colours, these dead structures take on a beauty of their own.

In gardens I design, I plan to use a good proportion of plants that I know will hold their structure when dead, for this reason. Often these plants have seed heads that are eaten by birds and small mammals, which again brings life to the garden in the dead months.

How to incorporate dead plants

It takes a leap from appreciating the structure of a seed head to considering it beautiful among colourful living flowers. Step back from a planting and think instead about structure and shape, how these contribute to the composition.

Dried dead seedheads can be part of an entirely new colour palette, coordinating best with whites, tawny oranges, crimsons and pinks. Try different combinations: I find dusky and pastel colours work best.

Through the season, as more plants die back and turn brown, the overall colour palette changes with multiple browns and beiges complementing each other. Grasses that turn brown work well alongside dried seedheads. If I plant something like an allium with the intention of leaving the seedhead through the year, I grow it next to a grass that I know will be brown too, or in the proximity of other plants that die back at the same time.

Opposite A mass of *Rudbeckia fulgida* var. *deamii* seed heads at the Sussex Prairies.

When to cut back

For wildlife's sake, try to leave as many dead plants to stand over winter as possible, cutting back only when they become very messy. Cut all the dead material back to ground level at the end of winter, as the weather starts to warm.

Looking for new growth in winter

Many people find the darkest months of winter depressing and gardens seem to grind to a halt, but this really isn't the case. It's surprising how much plants do grow in winter, and you can see this when you get down to their level. Throughout the chill of winter, roots can grow and buds swell, at ground level and on the branches of trees and shrubs. Thanks to the lack of leaves and stems, we're afforded a chance to see these minute advances.

A brighter future

By looking for shoots in winter and watching how they grow through the seasons, I can now recognise what is to come from this early growth. It's exciting and encouraging to see these stirrings and think of the plants that will emerge.

On a practical note, in this time you can evict any unwanted plants you recognise among the planting, lifting their roots out with your hori hori or hand fork. Some seedlings that I know don't mind being moved I lift carefully, without disturbing their roots, to plant in other areas.

Lending beautiful ecosystems a helping hand here and there in winter is for me as magical and refreshing as the cool air when I breathe it in deeply.

Above, left This mass of foxglove seedlings indicates the beautiful display to come in summer.
Above, right Choosing plants for their form when they die can create a structured, textural scene.

Plants for winter structure I've trialled

- *Achillea millefolium* – strong horizontal seed heads.
- *Cynara cardunculus* – cardoons are ornamental artichokes with huge thistle flowers that stand in winter.
- *Dipsacus fullonum* – teasel seed heads form good winter silhouettes.
- *Echinacea* spp. – the central black seed head is darker than most.
- *Helenium* spp. – smaller than *Echinacea* but with attractive black seed heads.
- *Hylotelephium spectabile* – similar to achillea with horizontal seed heads.
- *Lilium martagon* – seed pods on bare stems look like rattles (and do indeed rattle!).
- *Lunaria annua* – oval papery seed pods.
- *Miscanthus* spp. – grasses with excellent winter staying power.
- *Monarda* spp. – brown seed heads on bare stems.
- *Papaver somniferum* – classic and large poppy seed heads.
- *Pennisetum* – as with many ornamental grasses, the seed heads hold for most of winter.
- *Phlomis russeliana* – the flowers and leaves die back, leaving tall stems with layers of repeating seed heads.
- *Verbena bonariensis* – the bare stems hold the seed heads high above the ground.

Top A sea of dried *Allium cristophii* seed heads, which flowered in spring, blend with muted colours of *Hylotelephium* 'Matrona' flowering in autumn.
Middle, left *Echinacea pallida* seed heads.
Middle, right *Allium hollandicum* 'Purple Sensation' seed heads add structure alongside purple *Monarda didyma* 'Scorpion'.
Bottom *Eryngium giganteum* seed heads.

Don't forget the front

I love it when people grow plants outside front doors and in front gardens. It's a gesture for the local community to enjoy, always bringing a smile to my face and an uplift in mood. Watering our own pots out the front, I've been struck by how many of our neighbours stop by on their way to work or the shops. I've come to know them as friends. And these plants in our front gardens can be excellent pockets of food and habitat for wildlife such as bees.

Community benefits from plants

Whether your front garden is expansive or non-existent, there is always room to improve your local area and give something back to neighbours by adding a little green. A study by the University of Washington found all kinds of improvements in community behaviour and reductions in reported crime in greener neighbourhoods. Incident statistics showed that public housing buildings with more greenery experienced 52 per cent fewer crimes than buildings with little vegetation. In fact, all around the world, the greener the area, the more positive the people living in it are.

Many front gardens in urban areas are small and shaded. This can at first seem problematic, but is a prime opportunity for woodland planting. Not only incredibly beautiful, this kind of planting is great for wildlife owing to its density and often earlier flowering periods.

Door pots for visitors

What better way to thank your delivery driver, welcome guests or put a smile on your face on your way in or out than a pot of plants near the front door?

The bigger the pot the better it is for the plants, and it will retain more moisture than a small pot, reducing the need for you to water. A large pot 30–40cm (12–16in) wide gives you space to grow one key plant or a number of smaller plants together. You can also plant a few returning spring bulbs beneath the main plants for extra colour.

Place broken, curved pieces of old pots over the holes at the base of the pot to stop compost blocking them and help drainage. Then fill with peat-free compost mixed with about one fifth garden soil (or bought topsoil) for a mixed structure – you'll have both small

Opposite *Lavandula angustifolia*, *Bidens* 'Pirates Treasure', *Petunia* 'Double Yellow' mini trailing, *P.* 'Pastel Yellow', *Lotus maculata* 'Gold Flash' and *Helichrysum petiolare* 'Gold'.

Some of my favourite plants for pots

SHRUBS	PERENNIALS	BULBS	SUCCULENTS
Sun Brugmansia suaveolens Pinus wallichiana 'Nana' Salvia rosmarinus Other Salvia spp.	**Sun** Centranthus ruber 'Albus' and C. var. coccineus Pelargonium odoratissimum and P. sidoides Miscanthus 'Morning Light'	**Sun** Narcissus Nerine bowdenii Tulipa spp.	**Sun** Aeonium arboreum Echeveria elegans and E. secunda Hylotelephium 'Bertram Anderson' Sempervivum arachnoideum 'Minor', Sempervivum 'Brock' Sempervivum erythraeum
Part shade Fuchsia 'Hawkshead' Fuchsia 'Dying Embers' Fuchsia triphylla 'Mary' Hydrangea paniculata 'Little Lime'	**Part shade** Calamagrostis brachytricha Heuchera spp. Persicaria 'Purple Fantasy'	**ANNUALS** **Sun** Ammi majus and A. visnaga Cosmos bipinnatus	**CLIMBERS** **Sun** Clematis 'Avalanche' Passiflora 'White Lightning'
Full shade Mahonia eurybracteata subsp. ganpinensis 'Soft Caress'	**Full shade** Asplenium scolopendrium Begonia 'Benitochiba' Hakonechloa macra Pteris cretica 'Wimsettii'	**Part shade** Begonia rex Nicotiana alata and N. knightiana Solenostemon scutellarioides	**Full shade** Hedera helix 'Glacier' and 'Carolina Crinkle'

soil particles and larger organic material from the compost.

I like using medium and small grasses in pots: *Miscanthus sinensis* 'Morning Light' in sun, or *Calamagrostis brachytricha* and the smaller *Hakonechloa macra* 'All Gold' in shadier spots.

A small shrub has visual oomph and can prove more resilient to the drier conditions of pot life. The key with shrubs is to choose one that isn't moisture-loving and won't grow much more than 1.5m (5ft) otherwise it will be in danger of drying out. Shrubs such as *Mahonia eurybracteata* subsp. *ganpinensis* 'Soft Caress' grow well

in shade and *Hydrangea paniculata* 'Little Lime' will be happy in part to full shade. In sun, I've kept the large tree *Pinus nigra* as a small shrub by pinching the new growth (called candles) in half in spring, before the needles splay out.

Window boxes inside and out

Even if you've no garden at all, a window box outside and houseplants inside can form a substantial growing area. Given that windows are a prime focal point when looking at a house (or out of one), adding plants to them significantly increases the amount of green you see.

Above *Sedum* spp., *Echeveria* 'Perle von Nurnberg' and *Hylotelephium* 'Bertram Anderson'.

Use the largest and deepest window box you can find for good root space and moisture retention, filling it with peat-free compost. It's amazing how much you can grow in a window box, from dwarf tomato plants, aubergines and chillies to wildflowers for insects. A micro-meadow in a window box can help many insects.

I like to grow short succulents in the window boxes at the front of our house because it is roasted by the sun from midday until sunset. Using succulents seriously reduces the amount of watering required, which is good for me and for keeping my water usage sustainable.

Some of my favourite window-box plants

Sun
+ *Armeria maritima*
+ *Erigeron karvinskianus*
+ *Festuca amethystina*
+ *Lagurus ovatus*
+ *Lupinus nanus* 'Snow Pixie'
+ *Pelargonium sidoides*
+ *Verbena rigida*

Sun – very drought-tolerant
+ *Aeonium arboreum*
+ *Aloe aristata*
+ *Echeveria elegans, E. secunda* and *E.* 'Perle von Nurnberg'
+ *Hylotelephium* 'Bertram Anderson'
+ *Sempervivum* spp., including 'Brock' and *S. erythraeum*

Shade
+ *Heuchera* 'Green Tea'
+ *Polypodium cambricum* 'Cambricum'
+ *Solenostemon scutellarioides*

Four
Growing for wildlife

Early on in my gardening career, a white plume moth – ghostly with feathered, fragile wings, gliding like fluff – floated past me to perch on a blade of grass in the garden. As I stared at it I felt connected to the ecosystem that existed all around us, and a sense of meaning entered my life. I wondered what else I had overlooked.

I began noticing centipedes that lived under pots and tiny wrens that stalked the ivy for caterpillars. The way I gardened changed. Everything I did took into consideration the need to provide habitats for wildlife, nooks and crannies for bees and ladybirds to hibernate in, water for pond skaters and frogs, plants left through winter to give shelter for insects.

Birds, butterflies and hoverflies are as beautiful as flowers, and I design gardens with their contribution in mind. To make wildlife happy is easy; we simply need to understand their habitats and ecosystem, and they will reward us in return.

Creating a wildlife-friendly garden

I'm often surprised at how a couple of minutes watching wildlife can turn into a couple of hours. That's not time wasted; it helps us learn what those insects and animals need, informs future decisions about our gardens and gives us insights to share with others. Make time to slow down and watch what insects and other wildlife get up to. Observing their behaviour can be a captivating and mindful exercise.

Build connectedness by building habitats

Getting wildlife gardening right can generate a strong feeling of connectedness with nature. This is because an action we take, such as growing a plant or establishing a certain habitat, can have almost immediate visible results. A bee will visit the flower of a plant as soon as I've planted it; frogs and newts will appear in my allotment's pond within days of filling it with water. Long-term, the health of the ecosystem improves each year, creating a deeper sense of satisfaction and connection.

In addition, there is a deep satisfaction in knowing I've helped wildlife in a time of climate crisis, when it needs all the support it can get. The plants we grow, the habitats we encourage and our refusal to use pesticides ... all these things can make a big difference to thousands of little lives around us.

Planting for wildlife

I consider the value to wildlife of every plant I choose for garden designs (see

page 50). It's not all about flowers for pollinators; every plant has a place on a sliding scale of usefulness for wildlife. It's best to have a good mix of different plant types that will attract and support the greatest number and diversity of animals and insects.

+ **Natural flowers:** many garden plants such as roses and dahlias have been

bred to have many more petals than the species originally had. Called doubles, these flowers' nectar-producing nectaries and pollen-producing filaments have been turned into petals, significantly reducing their usefulness for insects. I choose mainly single flowers, such as *Dahlia* 'Bishop of Canterbury', because they're easier for insects to access pollen and nectar for food.

✛ **Flower shape:** flowers come in a wide variety of shapes and sizes, such as tubes, spires of flowers, bells and flat-topped arrangements of hundreds of tiny flowers (called umbels). Some insects are shaped to forage from small, flat flowers, others from large, funnel-shaped ones. To attract a range of different insects, therefore, you need a range of flower shapes and sizes.

✛ **Attractiveness to insects:** some plants will be more attractive to insects than others for reasons that are invisible to us. For example, the amount of pollen and nectar a flower holds can differ between cultivars (only existing by human cultivation) of the same species: grow two different types of rose next to one another and you are likely to find one is more popular with bees than the other. Plants aren't usually sold based on the species or quantity of insects they support – the generic 'good for pollinators' label doesn't scratch the surface. Instead, it can be best to work it out yourself. I do my best David Attenborough impression and watch plants on sunny, warm and windless days to see which attract the most insects. Frequently I'll grow different cultivars of the same plant close together and later remove the ones I can see are the least insect-friendly.

✛ **Indigenous versus exotic:** it's always good to grow some plants that are indigenous to your area, meaning

Below To attract wildlife you need to provide the right habitats. Common frogs (*Rana temporaria*) need ponds for shelter and to reproduce.

mammals need not only flowers but foliage and roots too. Caterpillars need leaves to eat, and can be as picky about which ones. Grasses are an important food source for insects and herbivorous mammals. Below ground, roots of all plants grow every year like leaves and many die back in winter. Live and dead roots are an important source of food for soil organisms.

✛ **Structure for shelter:** the shapes and structures of plants are an important aspect of wildlife habitats. Tall, dense trees and shrubs are essential to protect nesting birds from predators, especially thorny ones like pyracantha and hawthorn. Cracks in their bark, as well as grasses and flower stems, are used by insects to overwinter in.

✛ **Winter food:** plants that produce berries or seed heads that remain intact throughout a long period of winter are important food sources for wildlife that is still active in those months, such as birds.

they evolved or arrived in your region without the help of humans (you can identify them using a wildflower field guide). These plants evolved alongside the local wildlife. Some insects can physically feed on only a single species of plant, which makes this important. However, some exotic plants will be used by other local wildlife, including those introduced so many centuries ago they can almost be classified as indigenous themselves. The majority of insects are generalists, foraging from a wide variety of plants and happily using exotics they can access.

✛ **Foliage and roots:** insects, birds and

Bring soil to life

If the sun is our power source, soil is the giant battery pack enabling all plants on earth to grow. Healthy plants start with healthy soil, and that requires familiar subterranean wildlife such as worms and centipedes, as well as some creatures that may be unknown to you. What you do to protect the soil makes all the difference.

What wildlife uses the soil?

It may come as a surprise that, according to the Soil Association, 25 per cent of all species on earth live in soils, forming vital connections with the rest of life above ground. We're all familiar with earthworms and moles, but there are many other lesser-known life forms including microscopic worm-like nematodes, single-celled protozoa and bacteria.

The majority of these organisms serve an important role in breaking down dead plant and animal material, known as organic matter, releasing the nutrients locked in it for plant roots to absorb.

They also create a healthy structure for the soil, with a good mix of air pockets and clumps of earth, both of which are needed for roots to breathe and grow well. Worms, for instance, create tunnels that roots can easily grow through, while their excretions bind soil particles together. Plus, of course, they are food for other wildlife – we all know how much birds love a juicy worm.

How to add organic matter to your soil

Soil-dwelling life forms need a constant supply of organic matter to eat. In the wild, plants shed leaves in autumn and, over time, stems and branches die, while animals leave faeces and their own bodies return to the earth when they die. All of this creates a blanket of natural organic matter that is broken down by fungi and bacteria or eaten by other organisms.

In our gardens we can replicate this by adding a 3–5cm (1–2in) layer of homemade garden or bought peat-free compost every year. Known as a mulch, it should ideally be applied between the end of autumn and the start of spring, but any time of year is fine. Just be careful to avoid burying tree trunks, plant stems or crowns (growing points of perennials found at ground level), which can cause them to rot.

Although gravel is sometimes referred to as a mulch – and it is one – it doesn't help plants in the same way because stone is inorganic and won't break down, though it can help to lock in moisture.

Benefits of leaf litter

Many people clear away fallen leaves and plant debris in their gardens, and it is important to do so if lawns or smaller plants are being smothered and starved of sunlight. However, I try to replicate nature by leaving or brushing fallen leaves and debris beneath ornamental plants as a natural mulch, to encourage wildlife and feed the soil.

What wildlife uses leaf litter?

Slugs and snails eat fallen leaves and dead plant material; it's one of their most important roles in the garden, breaking plant matter down into nutrient-rich faeces. Worms do the same, drawing leaves deeper into the soil. Arthropods (insects with a hard outer shell) including woodlice and millipedes are also detritivores, eating dead plant material. Nematodes, fungi and bacteria help to decompose it further.

All of this life is, in turn, food for other insects and arachnids such as beetles and spiders, as well as small animals including mice, birds, snakes and toads. Unfortunately, recommended garden practice in the past has been to clear up dead leaves, in order to reduce the slug populations and plant diseases that can be harboured in them. Yet fallen leaves are a vital habitat and food source for wildlife; by clearing them we remove these resources and damage our ecosystem.

In my urban garden, space is at a premium. We don't have room for a large compost bin as well as a leaf bin, so leaves stay on the ground. Despite a large silver birch and two plum trees dumping their leaves into our garden every autumn, I find that the wildlife breaks it all down before the end of winter. It's miraculous.

Controlling leaf diseases

If any plant develops a leaf disease in summer, such as powdery mildew (white dusting) or rust (orange spots), I make sure to remove the affected leaves, where practical, to control the problem. On larger trees this won't always be possible. Throw diseased leaves in the bin or burn them; don't put them on the compost heap, which keeps the problem in your garden.

Opposite It's important to remove fallen leaves from lawns to allow light to reach the grass, but in the border they become lost among the planting and create an important wildlife habitat.

Learn to love fallen leaves

I enjoy seeing these fallen leaves in autumn, not only for their colours but because they symbolise a key step in the circle of life. It's true that leaf litter will become home to slugs, which may be a problem in spring, when new shoots arrive. But there are two reasons why I don't mind this.

First, I design gardens with a strong visual structure, using simple paths, seating areas and evergreen plants and hedges to help frame and differentiate them from busy naturalistic planting. This structured layout will draw your eye to these elements and away from the mess of fallen leaves in winter, as long as the path or lawn itself is kept clear.

Second, letting leaves lie on the soil makes one of nature's great phenomena visible to us: the speed at which the leaves are broken down and absorbed into the soil, the great recycling. By spring, the soil is clear of leaves and the slugs aren't as big a problem as we might have thought back in autumn. I see this happen every year, and it connects me more closely to the seasons.

Some leaves can take longer to decompose, such as oak and evergreens, but this is a good thing, as they can be used as shelter by damp-loving species including toads and frogs in the hotter, drier months of summer. And toads and frogs eat slugs.

Compost bins: a wildlife haven

I'm obsessed with compost bins. I don't care how mad that sounds because I know that when you start composting you'll feel the same. Making compost is addictive and one of the best activities to help the planet, recycling plant waste into nutrient-rich compost to grow future plants, the essence of sustainability. What's more, the very process of making compost locks carbon back into our soil. And the bin is a Mecca for wildlife.

What wildlife uses compost bins?

I don't use sealed plastic or 'hot' compost bins (completely enclosed to increase temperature), because wildlife cannot access them. Insects such as beetles, bees and wasps, slugs, snails, centipedes, millipedes and many other creatures love compost heaps because they provide warm shelter and food to eat. Centipedes are among the most important of these in gardens because they eat insect pests and slugs. Larger animals such as hedgehogs love to shelter in compost bins too. Great care should be taken before sticking tools into compost bins for this reason.

After a number of years, insects that eat dead wood will slowly nibble and break down the wooden structure of the compost bin itself. Wasps will scrape it to make nests and beetle larvae feed on decaying bits. It means even the bin itself is recyclable, and will need to be replaced every five to ten years or so.

Dissuade mice and rats by lining the inside and base with a strong metal mesh – they can gnaw through chicken wire.

Only add plant material from the garden and uncooked vegetables, not smelly cooked food.

How to make a compost bin

1. Find enough untreated planks of wood to make each bin at least 1m (3ft) wide × 1m tall × 1m deep. Untreated wood is best, because although treated wood lasts longer, it can leach chemicals into the compost and soil, and the wood itself won't decompose for many years. Upcycle wood from things like pallets and old furniture.
2. Use four strong wooden posts to form the corners.
3. Your upcycled wood forms the side bars. Keep gaps between the pieces of wood of at least 3cm (just over 1in) for good airflow, essential for decomposition.
4. Nail or screw it all together.
5. Make one side of the bin lower or detachable to give you easier access for turning and removing the eventual compost.

Don't have room for a compost bin?

We only have room for a small compost bin, so I finely chop most of our plant waste using my secateurs and shears, spreading the tiny pieces over the soil. They are soon incorporated into the ground naturally by organisms, alongside leaf litter. It's the same process as making compost, except by spreading it across the ground rather than gathering it into a convenient bin.

How to make compost

Here are the key rules for successful composting.

✛ **Layer:** good compost is made from roughly one third green plant waste (fresh leaves, flowers and stems) to two thirds brown plant waste (dead or woody material). Green waste provides moisture and brown provides structure. Add both in rough layers like a lasagne. All plant waste decomposes eventually, but having the right ratio will speed up the process – experiment to find what works for you. If you don't have enough brown waste, add brown cardboard. Add water if the mix feels dry.

✛ **Chop:** always chop plants into the smallest pieces you can. I aim for everything to be 10cm (4in) long or less. The smaller the pieces, the faster they decompose. With tougher brown material it is important to expose a greater surface area, speeding things up. Preparing large woody stems (more than 1cm/½in in diameter) will need a shredder, though I've lived without one.

✛ **Turn:** as in baking, turn the compost using a garden fork to mix everything together. Compost decomposes fastest in the middle, where it is warmest, and by turning it you can make sure everything has its time in the hot spot. I turn my compost every few months.

✛ **Wait:** it takes time for microorganisms to work their magic on compost, though I usually find my heap has turned into crumbly compost after six to nine months and a couple of turns. This can happen much faster with larger heaps and more frequent turning.

Dead wood habitats

If a tree or shrub dies or is cut down in your garden, rather than remove the dead wood, keep it as a vital habitat and food source for wildlife in your ecosystem. You may even find new and stylish ways to incorporate it as part of your garden design.

What wildlife uses dead wood?

Trees and shrubs form woody material in their trunks and branches, made from different cells to those in soft green growth. A number of different groups of cells are toughened by a substance called lignin, giving wood its strength. Different tree species are denser and harder than others, which is why oak is called a hardwood and pine a softwood, for example.

Dead wood, whether part of a living tree or separate from it, is particularly useful to wildlife because it becomes easier to burrow into or eat as it decomposes. Over millions of years insects, animals and fungi have evolved alongside woody plants, and hundreds of thousands of species need wood to live.

For instance, there are over 1,200 species of stag beetle around the world, and in Europe the larvae of one of these, *Lucanus cervus* (which is locally endangered), feed on decaying wood. Incredibly, this large but harmless insect spends most of its life below ground or in decaying tree stumps as a large larva; it can live between four and seven years, but the beetle stage spent above ground is only a few short months long. Decaying wood left untouched for many years is therefore essential for its survival.

The same is true of thousands of other species of insect and animal, all of which are connected to the wider ecosystem. Insect larvae break down the wood to return nutrients to the soil for plants, and serve as food for larger animals around the world, from woodpeckers to racoons and chimpanzees.

Living trees can develop sections of dead or decaying wood when branches are damaged or simply as a result of age or disease. Often these form hollows as they decay or are carved into by animals. Squirrels, bats and birds will sleep and breed in these hollows, after they create or find them.

How to make a stylish dead wood habitat

Adding a log pile in the corner of the garden is an easy way to instantly benefit wildlife. There it will slowly decay, providing food and shelter for insects and mammals for years. In small gardens

this can be tricky because everything is on show. While I always approach these issues putting wildlife first, it's possible to think of ways to use dead wood in gardens in a more stylish way.

Stacking cut wood neatly into piles can look decorative, or you can create a loggery, treating upright logs as statuesque forms dotted through plants. I created a loggery for beetles from segments of a pollarded tree branch from our local Eden Community Garden in South London. The bottom third of each log was buried in the soil for stability and, importantly, to aid the decomposition process, the wood having contact with soil organisms and moisture. They looked attractive in their own right, but I decided to add a contemporary touch by using a soldering iron to burn some patterns on to the exposed ends. The patterns won't last forever but make for a striking feature.

In some gardens I've seen shrubs with strong structures that have died and have been left standing. As the bark peels off the bare wood it takes on a light grey, almost bone-like appearance that looks good among buff ornamental grasses. Birds use bare stems like this to perch on.

Above Dead wood can make a valuable wildlife habitat; be creative with how to incorporate it into your garden. Here I've used a soldering iron to create a pattern on the logs, but you could carve a design instead to make a unique sculpture.

Grassland in the garden

Wild grasslands can be home to as many as thirty flowering plant species per quarter of a square metre (3sq. ft), evolving to grow tightly packed among grasses in a dense plant community. This rich habitat is home to a huge range of wildlife and is easy to incorporate into gardens, no matter how small. An area of grassland has a relaxing air of lightness, capturing the movement of wind and lifting mood.

What wildlife uses grassland?

Grasslands form in areas with little rainfall or shallow soils, preventing the growth of trees that might shade out the sun-loving grassland species. They have different names around the world, including Eurasian steppe, North American prairie and African savannah. Meadows are mostly human-made grassland and are only semi-wild, because they rely on us cutting back annually and preventing shrubs and trees from taking hold. All are used by a vast and complex web of life.

The most visible users are pollinating insects visiting flowers, such as butterflies, bees, hoverflies and moths. But many of these also feed on the grass leaves in their less visible caterpillar or larval phase, as well as on the leaves of other plants. In gardens, grasses left over winter provide shelter for insects such as ladybirds. As their name suggests, grasshoppers thrive in this habitat; as herbivores they eat plants including grasses and lay eggs in soil beneath the vegetation.

Spiders form webs between the strong stems of grasses and other tough grassland plants, and mammals such as mice feed on seeds. Reptiles including snakes and lizards prey on insects and small mammals in the grassland, while soil-dwelling species such as worms and ground bees make burrows between grass roots.

Birds in turn feed on the insects, reptiles and mammals living among grasses and incorporate blades of grass in their nests. Ground-nesting birds use grasses as shelter while they raise their young, though in gardens you'll need a very large area for them to feel safe enough to do this. In the wild, larger herbivorous mammals such as deer feed on grassland plants too.

Opposite A garden grassland area is made more colourful with swathes of Verbena bonariensis. The flowers grab our attention but the tufts of grass leaves are just as important to wildlife for food and shelter.

Above *Vicia cracca* (tufted vetch) and Yorkshire fog grass, *Holcus lanatus*, growing together naturally in a meadow.

How to grow a mini grassland

In a garden you don't need a large grassland to benefit wildlife. One or two grasses make an instant impact as insects will be able to feed off them and use them for shelter, bees make nests beneath them and birds collect nesting material. There are true grasses and near identical-looking plants called sedges and rushes; they are all useful and I'll discuss them together here as grasses. Some will be evergreen, others deciduous, though even these usually hold their shape for most of winter. It's almost always best to leave grasses uncut through winter for wildlife, only cutting back brown deciduous leaves in early spring, which is also a good time to cut back evergreen grasses if they look a bit tatty. Meadows are an exception (see right). Here are a few different types of grassland you can grow in your garden:

✢ **Steppe and prairie:** I use a lot of steppe and prairie grasses as framework or star plants (see pp.55, 58) in gardens because I find them very beautiful; their wildlife value is a bonus. Non-indigenous grasses from different parts of the world can still provide shelter for wildlife and nesting material, and may be eaten, particularly if they share the qualities of indigenous species in your area. But it's worth including some indigenous species too, because these are likely to help indigenous insects.

✢ **Meadows:** turning an area of your garden into a meadow is a beautiful way to help wildlife. You can leave weedy lawns to grow naturally or add seeds to them in autumn. It's best to buy seeds harvested from grasslands near you to benefit local wildlife, and you must rake the lawn heavily to expose soil for them (a process called scarifying). Fertility of the soil doesn't matter because meadows naturally occur on nutrient-rich and poor soils, but it will dictate the plants you grow depending on the conditions they prefer. Meadows require cutting two or three times a year, usually in early spring, midsummer – after seeds have fallen from plants – and autumn.

✤ **Lawns:** even a neatly mown lawn has wildlife value. It is useful for subterranean beasties like worms that are eaten by birds, and short grass is actually necessary for burrowing solitary bees and leatherjackets (crane fly larvae). You can make the lawn more valuable for wildlife by allowing some flowering plants in it. I encourage them because I prefer the look of a lawn dotted with daisies (*Bellis perennis*), dove's-foot cranesbill (*Geranium molle*) and self-heal (*Prunella vulgaris*). The charity Plantlife found that lawns mown less regularly – every four weeks – attracted ten times the number of bees because lawn plants had a better chance of flowering.

✤ **Grasses in pots:** many grasses will be happy in pots of the correct size. For instance, I've grown *Festuca amethystina* in window boxes and both *Miscanthus sinensis* 'Morning Light' and *Deschampsia cespitosa* in large pots (30cm/12in wide × 30cm deep) of peat-free compost.

Some of my favourite grasses

✤ *Calamagrostis* × *acutiflora* 'Karl Foerster' – sun, medium
✤ *Calamagrostis brachytricha* – part-shade, medium
✤ *Carex grayii* – part-shade, small
✤ *Deschampsia cespitosa* – sun, small
✤ *Hakonechloa macra* – shade, small
✤ *Jarava ichu* – sun, medium
✤ *Miscanthus giganteus* – sun, large
✤ *Miscanthus sinensis* 'Gracillimus' and 'Morning Light' – sun, large
✤ *Panicum* 'Northwind' – sun, medium

Above Calamagrostis brachytricha among late-flowering Symphyotrichum amellus 'King George' and S. novae-angliae 'violetta' with the grass Jarava ichu in the background.

Growing for wildlife / 101

Welcoming pond life

Water is vital for all life, so it comes as no surprise that a pond is an essential means of helping wildlife in the garden. Around the world, freshwater ponds are in significant decline, many having been removed in the last century in urban and farming areas. Be a wildlife superhero, and add a pond to your plot. You don't need a huge space – a balcony will do.

What wildlife uses ponds?

Rumbles, our cat, saw our micro pond as a giant water bowl, and he wasn't the only one. It was home to pond skaters (*Gerris lacustris*), lesser water boatmen (*Corixa punctata*) and damselflies, and all the birds and other insects in the neighbourhood visited for a drink. You may find that common frogs (*Rana temporaria*), toads (*Bufo bufo*), smooth newts (*Lissotriton vulgaris*), dragonflies, water snails and an amazing array of new species will flock to your garden. Mammals and reptiles will drink from ponds too, such as hedgehogs (*Erinaceus europaeus*), polecats (*Mustela putorius*), roe deer (*Capreolus capreolus*) and grass snakes (*Natrix natrix*).

For your own wellbeing, you can't beat a water feature either. Watching pond life is captivating, as are the raindrops rippling and light shimmering on the surface. I love microponds so much that I added two permanent ones as the central feature of our little garden. Contrary to popular belief, they're the easiest thing to look after if you follow nature's rules.

Above The ponds contain dwarf waterlily Nymphaea 'Laydekeri Fulgens' and Ceratophyllum demersum.

How to make a micropond

❶ Choose a container or dig a hole at least 60 × 60cm (24 × 24in) and preferably 30–40cm (12–16in) deep.
❷ Make sure one side is sloping or add a wooden ramp for wildlife to get out.
❸ Position your pond in partial shade. This will allow pond plants to grow

while preventing the pond from overheating and algae taking hold, which happens in full sun.

4 If digging a hole, line it with sharp sand (to protect the liner from jagged stones) and a butyl pond liner, allowing an extra 30cm (12in) to overhang the edge of the hole. Fill the pond with water to stretch the liner out before tucking the overhang under soil or rocks.

5 Ideally, fill the pond with rainwater, though realistically, most people have to use tap water. Leave for 24 hours for chemicals like chlorine to reduce before adding plants.

6 Add underwater oxygenating plants if the pond is at least 30cm (12in) deep. I use *Ceratophyllum demersum*.

7 Pond plants can then be added in specialist basket pots using aquatic compost (which is peat-free as standard), topped with gravel to keep the soil in. Make sure they are placed at the correct depth. Miniature water lilies go on the bottom, at 30cm (12in) or deeper. I grow *Nymphaea* 'Laydekeri Fulgens'.

8 Marginal plants sit at shallower depths, with only 2–5cm (1–2in) of water over the top of the basket and soil. Rest them on bricks or upside-down pots to raise them. I have found *Iris* 'Black Gamecock' and *Cyperus involucratus* grow well.

Above Adding oxygenating *Myriophyllum spicatum* alongside part-shade micropond plants *Anemopsis californica, Cyperus involucratus* and *Myosotis sylvatica* 'Alba'.

Top tips for water features
- New ponds can turn green with algae while everything settles in – caused by excess nitrogen. Eventually your plants will absorb it and the water will clear a little. If it doesn't, add an extra plant or two, or a small bundle of barley straw.
- Mosquitoes can be a problem. I've found a weekly scoop with a small fish net reduces the number of larvae in small ponds. Pond skaters, frogs and newts will also eat the larvae, keeping them under control. It's worth holding out for this wildlife to arrive. If the problem is particularly bad, you can add small fish to eat the mosquito larvae, but they will eat other insect life too, and make the water dirty.

Attract and sustain insect life in your garden

According to the Wildlife Trusts, 41 per cent of insects around the world are threatened with extinction caused by habitat loss, monocultures in farming, and insecticide use. With such pressure on insects, your garden can prove a lifeline for key species that provide food for birds and mammals.

Welcome awesome aphids

Realising how important aphids are to other wildlife changed everything for me. I used to worry about aphids damaging plants or spreading viruses; now I'm excited to see them because they are a cornerstone species – the more aphids, the more wildlife diversity.

Did you know?

Around the world there are over 4,000 known species of aphid in the family Aphididae, and, although to human eyes they look similar, many aphid species are reliant on specific plants, though some are less picky. Aphids feed by sucking plant sap through a syringe-like stylet.

In our garden we have a wide range of aphid species, including greenfly known as potato aphids (*Macrosiphum euphorbiae*), blackfly (*Aphis fabae*), woolly aphids (*Eriosoma lanigerum*), grey pine needle aphids (*Schizolachnus pineti*), chunky hellebore aphids (*M. hellebori*) and whopper lupin aphids (*M. albifrons*).

Opposite A leafcutter bee, *Megachile willughbiella*, on *Helenium* 'Moerheim Beauty'.

Aphids have a remarkable relationship with some ant species (garden ants are entirely harmless). Ants pick aphids up with their super-ant strength, carrying them to succulent plant shoots, where they farm them like green alien sheep in miniature. The ants eat the sticky, sugary honeydew that the aphids secrete. Yes, ants farm and eat aphid poo. In our garden I watch black ants (*Lasius niger*) shepherding aphids around our elderflower shrub, *Sambucus nigra* f. *porphyrophylla* 'Black Lace'.

Aphids are particularly notable because of the way they reproduce. While they can and do mate, far more aphids are born via parthenogenesis, which is asexual fertilisation of eggs by females. These offspring are female clones that hatch inside the mother and are then born live, a process called vivipary. Over winter they'll move to woody shrubs and trees, but in spring and summer they return to softer herbaceous plants where population numbers increase exponentially. Unchecked, one female aphid could produce millions if not billions of offspring in a single season.

What eats aphids?

The good news – for us, not so much for the aphids – is that they're food to almost all the friendliest garden wildlife. Small birds such as blue tits, great tits, coal tits, long-tailed tits, wrens, robins and dunnocks all eat them, especially those on shoots of early-blossoming fruit trees. Earwigs also eat aphids, while parasitic wasps lay eggs into the aphids themselves, so killing them. Brightly coloured ladybirds, hoverflies and emerald-green lacewings all set about devouring them, especially in their voracious larval stages. Without aphids gardens wouldn't have so many of these wonderful creatures.

Above Marmalade hoverfly, *Episyrphus balteatus*, on Aster *amellus* 'Veilchenkönigin'.

How to control aphids

After a year or two I found that ladybirds, hoverflies and birds polish off all aphids in our garden, so I don't have to. When they're particularly numerous, you can squish them with your fingers, wipe them away from plants or wash them off gently with a hose.

Hang around with hoverflies

Who wouldn't love to hover about as hoverflies do? Hoverflies were among the first insects I felt a connection to in our garden; I like the way they hang in the air at eye level, keeping me company.

While many people spend time getting rid of aphids, I actively farm them as a buffet to attract hoverflies. It requires nerve waiting for hoverfly larvae to hatch, but they then make short work of the bugs. Spraying aphids with chemicals leaves hoverflies that eat them to starve or, worse, kills them and other beneficial insects.

Plants to attract hoverflies

Flat-topped umbels are clusters of many tiny flowers held together on short stems. They are loved by hoverflies, which use them like landing pads.

Above Any container with stagnant water and rotting plant material will soon become home to hoverfly larvae.

Umbels are seen on astrantias, fennel (*Foeniculum vulgare*), yarrow (*Achillea* spp.), wild carrot (*Daucus carota*) and *Ammi visnaga*, though hoverflies use many other flowers too, including hawthorn (*Crataegus monogyna*) and oxeye daisy (*Leucanthemum vulgare*).

How to make a hoverfly hot tub

Some hoverfly species lay eggs on plants, in the nests of other insects or in the bark of trees. A few species need a little helping hand, however, because they reproduce in stagnant water, the kind that is full of decomposing leaf matter. It creates a bit of a stench but they love it! Eggs laid in the water hatch into larvae with long tail-like organs for breathing; they are not really tails, but give the larvae the name rat-tailed maggots. Eventually these pupate, becoming zippy hoverflies.

1. Take a watertight container roughly 15cm (6in) wide and deep (or larger). It can be made from anything, but I've chosen a ceramic pot without drainage holes to make it slightly more attractive to human eyes.
2. Add enough leaves to almost fill it but leaving room for plenty of water.
3. Also add a couple of sticks for the hoverflies to climb out on when mature.
4. Place in a shady corner away from human noses, and leave.
5. After a number of weeks you can gently root around in the water to see if you can find any of the strange-looking larvae, but be careful as they're very fragile.

Help bees and wasps

There are over 20,000 bee species
around the world, more than 2,000 of
them in Europe. These numbers are
staggering, until you consider that there
are a whopping 150,000 species of
wasp! They come in all shapes, colours
and sizes and play critical roles in many
ecosystems, from pollination to eating
problem insects. Bees and wasps need
our help, and our gardens are a perfect
home for our buzzy friends.

Did you know?

Bees and wasps evolved from the
same ancestors millions of years ago
and are closely related to ants and
sawflies. They belong to the scientific
family Hymenoptera: the name means
'membranous wings', which they all have,
except for some ants.

Many are endangered because humans
continue to destroy their habitats for
buildings and farming, and because of the
mass use of pesticides. Despite honeybees
receiving the limelight because of their
importance as crop pollinators and honey
producers, they are not endangered. It's
the thousands of other bees and wasps
we need to worry about. As I've explored
their world, I've been in awe of the array of
amazing appearances and behaviours they
exhibit.

Not all bees and wasps build and live
socially in hives; others can be solitary,
spending their lives alone except to mate.
Some of these create nests in holes and
dig burrows, such as the wool carder bee
(*Anthidium manicatum*), ashy mining bee
(*Adrena cineraria*) and field-digger wasps
(*Mellinus arvensis*). A number of bees and
wasps are parasites, such as the beautiful
solitary wasp, *Gasteruption jaculator*,
laying their eggs in the nests of others.

Not all bees make honey, nor do all
bees and wasps sting. Male honey bees
(*Apis mellifera*) and male bumblebees,
such as the red-tailed bumblebee (*Bombus
lapidarius*), don't have stings. Female
bumblebees are unlikely to sting unless
provoked, and they raise their legs to warn
you off first!

Different species are active in different months; the hairy-footed flower bee (*Anthophora plumipes*) is one of the first you'll see in spring, while the buff-tailed bumblebee (*Bombus terrestris*) is active throughout winter. To boost the appeal of your garden to different bees and wasps, keep an eye out to see which plants they prefer to visit, and steer your planting towards those that are most beneficial.

Build a solitary bee house

1. Use a block of untreated wood at least 15–20cm (6–8in)deep. It must be untreated, otherwise the anti-fungicidal and -bacterial chemicals the wood is injected with could be harmful to the bees and wasps.

2. Drill holes in the block using different diameter bits between 2 and 10mm. They need to be long drill bits to make holes that are 15cm (6in) deep, because solitary bees like to feel safe from birds, as far into the wood as possible.

3. Try to angle the holes ever so slightly upwards for rain to drain out.

4. Smooth the entrances with sandpaper.

5. Consider adding a little wooden roof that juts out by a finger width from the front of the block to keep rainwater out of the holes; damp can cause fungal or bacterial problems. My bee house is positioned under the eaves of my own house, achieving the same thing.

6. Alternatively, cut 15cm (6in) lengths of bamboo with a mix of diameters. Pack them together in a wooden box with a solid back but an open front, and a 1–2cm (½–¾in) overhang on the top to protect from rain.

7. Attach the box to a sunny south-facing wall or fence (north-facing in the southern hemisphere) for warmth, approximately 1m (3ft) from the ground.

8. You'll see solitary bees using the house in winter. Replace the wood or bamboo in summer each year for cleanliness, recycling the old block in your dead wood habitat (p.96).

Above Buff-tailed bumblebee, *Bombus terrestris*, can easily access the single flowers of *Dahlia* 'Bishop of Canterbury'.

Give bees a grassy knoll

Short-mown turf can be used by ground-nesting bees that like to dig burrows in soil. This will often be on sunny south-facing slopes for warmth (north-facing in the southern hemisphere).

Clump-forming ornamental grasses create a mound, and their roots make a perfect place for solitary bees to burrow. I use *Deschampsia cespitosa* and *Molinia caerulea*, indigenous to where I live.

Grow bee- and wasp-friendly plants

Any plant with natural, single flowers, as opposed to highly bred 'doubles' (see p.88–89), will attract and benefit bees, wasps and other pollinators. Wasps tend to feed on other insects, such as aphids, but will also use nectar. Include a mix of shapes and colours to suit different species that have various lengths and shapes of tongue.

Long-tongued bumblebees are able to use larger bell-shaped flowers, whereas short-tongued insects, including the common wasp (*Vespula vulgaris*) and the brassy mining bee (*Lasioglossum morio*), need the likes of daisies, persicaria and umbels with many tiny flowers held in a single flowerhead (inflorescence).

Occasionally short-tongued bees will make holes at the base of long-tubed flowers to 'rob nectar' from the flower without pollinating it. I see buff-tailed bumblebees doing this to salvias in our garden, and the holes are then also used by honey bees.

Only buy plants from stores that guarantee no chemicals have been used on them, as pesticide-treated plants harm or kill insects. Otherwise, grow your own from seeds or cuttings (p.38–43).

Some plants I grow for bees and wasps:
+ *Achillea millefolium*
+ *Allium* spp.
+ *Astrantia major*
+ *Borago officinalis*
+ *Centaurea nigra*
+ *Cerinthe major* 'Purpurescens'
+ *Dahlia* spp.
+ *Digitalis purpurea*
+ *Echinacea* spp.
+ *Foeniculum vulgare*
+ *Hellebore* spp.
+ *Lamium album*
+ *Lamium purpureum*
+ *Leucanthemum vulgare*
+ *Malus domestica* (apple)
+ *Persicaria amplexicaulis*
+ *Phacelia tanacetifolia*
+ *Salvia* spp.
+ *Trifolium pratense* (clover)

Above Common European garden spider, Araneus diadematus, is harmless and helpful, with beautiful stripes.

Spare the spiders

It may give you the creeps simply to have this page open if you are an arachnophobe. I include myself here; I am scared of spiders, but gradually I have overcome this fear somewhat by paying more attention to them, discovering spiders are the good guys. Some species, such as the European common garden spider (*Araneus diadematus*), are actually quite slow and gentle, helpfully eat problem insects, and are very beautiful.

Did you know?

There are almost 50,000 spider species around the world and not one of them wants to attack humans; most aren't even capable of biting us. Spiders can be tiny or large, colourful to stand out like the wasp spider (*Argiope bruennichi*) or camouflaged to blend into their surroundings. Some hunting spiders, such as white crab spiders (*Thomisus spectabilis*), lurk in the petals of flowers ready to pounce on unwitting pollinators!

Some produce the familiar webs to catch flying insects, others live in cracks and holes in walls and use strands of web to detect movement nearby. A few are more active, running or jumping about as they hunt small insects.

Spiders are essential predators in ecosystems because they keep other insects in check. In gardens they help achieve a balance with insects that eat plants (or us, thinking of mosquitoes). On the flip side, spiders are lunch for birds.

How to help spiders

Many web-building garden spiders do so 30–200cm (12–80in) above the ground, where insects fly (some will go higher into trees and shrubs). The best plants for webs are those with tall, sturdy and narrow stems that branch slightly but have an open form allowing insects to fly through. Importantly, they must be sturdy enough to stay standing in autumn and early winter (see p.79). Use sturdy perennials such as the ornamental grasses *Calamagrostis*, *Miscanthus* and *Molinia*, which are tall and open, just right for web building. Flowers with open structure include *Monarda*, *Veronicastrum* and thistles such as *Cardunculus*, *Centaurea* and *Cirsium*. Shrubs with an open, airy structure are good for spiders too, including buddleias, roses and most deciduous shrubs.

Leave leaf litter for spiders to shelter in from hot sun, rain and predators such as birds.

Be good to butterflies and moths

Not wanting to do butterflies a disservice – they're stunning, after all – but I really love moths. I noticed early on that our garden is a haven for them, and once I stopped to look at them closely I saw how fluffy and patterned moths are, in cool earth tones and khaki camo. Alongside birds, I view butterflies and moths as one more visual element of a garden and plan to attract as many as possible.

How to attract moths and butterflies

When I first started gardening I would pick caterpillars off plants to stop them eating them, while also planting flowers to attract more butterflies. Now I see how ridiculous this is. All butterflies and moths start life as a caterpillar, so removing them reduced the numbers of the very creatures I wanted to attract.

I want to bring all types of butterflies and moths to the garden, not only the showiest, but if you'd like to attract certain types, look to the plants their caterpillars eat. Many feed on plants we think of as weeds, while others depend on grasses. Most are very particular, only eating certain species of plant. Research your favourite local species online to see what plants they need. One tip is to ensure your lawn uses mainly grasses that are indigenous to your region.

Once caterpillars pupate and re-emerge as butterflies or moths, they can be more generalist in the plants they eat, though some still feed only on one particular plant species. Butterflies usually have small tongues and drink nectar from small flowers grouped together en masse, as found on the well-named butterfly bush, buddleia, and on achilleas.

Opposite Six-spot burnet moth, *Zygaena filipendulae*, on common knapweed, *Centaurea nigra*.
Below, left White plume moth, *Pterophorus pentadactyla*.
Below, right Caterpillar of the knot grass moth, *Acronicta rumicis*, on flower stalks.

Moths are similar, though many have longer tongues that unravel, able to reach into deeper tubular flowers, as found on *Nicotiana alata*. Some plants such as *Nicotiana* and *Lonicera* (honeysuckle), evolved to attract night-flying moths using strong evening scent and white or pale flowers that glow in moonlight.

Study moths with a moth trap

Daytime butterflies are easy to see. Moths largely fly at dusk or at night, and even the daytime moths dive for cover quickly to avoid birds. To catch them you can use expensive dedicated moth traps, but equally good is a bright light behind a white sheet. They'll fly into this at night, where you can softly scoop them up in a net to look at.

Some plants for caterpillars to eat

✢ The common blue (*Polyommatus icarus*) and silver-studded blue butterfly (*Plebejus argus*) are both threatened in the wild, but we can help them by growing yellow-flowered *Lotus corniculatus* (bird's-foot trefoil), which their caterpillars feed on. While the common stinging nettle, *Urtica dioica*, is the favourite caterpillar food of many moths and butterflies including the small tortoiseshell (*Aglais urticae*),

red admiral (*Vanessa atalanta*) and peacock butterfly (*Aglais io*).

✢ *Salix caprea* (goat/pussy willow) isn't the most beautiful plant but is vital to the caterpillars of the threatened purple emperor butterfly (*Apatura iris*). Common ivy, *Hedera helix*, and holly, *Ilex* spp., are incredibly useful for wildlife including birds, bees and spiders, and both are important food for holly blue butterfly caterpillars (*Celastrina argiolus*).

✢ Striking burnished brass moth (*Diachrysia chrysitis*) caterpillars feed on thistles (*Cirsium vulgare*), stinging nettles and white dead nettle (*Lamium album*).

✢ The red and black cinnabar moth's caterpillars primarily feed on the yellow wildflower ragwort (*Tyria jacobaeae*), alongside over 200 other insect species.

Above left Dark green fritillary butterfly, Speyeria aglaja, nectaring on field scabious, Knautia arvensis.
Above right Small purple and gold moth, Pyrausta aurata, managing to find some pollen in Dahlia 'Moor Place'.

Flowers enjoyed by butterflies and moths

Trees and shrubs
- *Buddleia* spp.
- *Ceanothus* spp.
- *Crataegus monogyna* (hawthorn)
- *Hebe* spp.
- *Malus domestica* (apple)
- *Prunus domestica* (plum)
- *Prunus* spp. (cherry)
- *Salvia rosmarinus* (rosemary)
- *Salvia* spp. (sages)

Annuals and biennials
- *Calendula officinalis* (pot marigold)
- *Centaurea cyanus*
- *Cosmos bipinnatus*
- *Dipsacus fullonum* (teasel)
- *Eryngium* spp.
- *Lunaria annua* (honesty)
- *Silene dioica* (red campion)
- *Trifolium* spp. (clover)

Perennials
- *Cynara cardunculus* (globe artichoke)
- *Dahlia* spp. (single-flowered)
- *Foeniculum vulgare* (fennel)
- *Geranium* spp.
- *Hyacinthoides non-scripta* (bluebell)
- *Hylotelephium* spp. (sedum)
- *Mentha* spp. (mints)
- *Origanum vulgare* (wild marjoram)
- *Pulmonaria* spp.
- *Symphyotrichum* spp. (asters)
- *Symphytum* spp. (comfrey)
- *Verbena bonariensis*

Grasses
- *Agrostis* spp.
- *Dactylis glomerata*
- *Festuca ovina*
- *Festuca rubra*
- *Holcus lanatus*

Evening-scented flowers for night moths
- *Lonicera* spp. (honeysuckle)
- *Nicotiana alata*
- *Oenothera* spp. (evening primrose)
- *Trachelospermum jasminoides* (star jasmine)

Top Hyacinthoides non-scripta, bluebells.
Middle Hebe 'Wiri Joy'.
Bottom Dahlia grown from seed.

Encourage birds and mammals to your garden

According to the Living Planet Report 2020 by WWF and the Zoological Society of London, there was a decrease of 68% in mammals, birds, amphibians, reptiles and fish between 1970 and 2016. In a time when scientists report that only 23.2% of the earth's surface is still truly wild habitat, decreasing by approximately 9.6% in two decades, welcoming birds and mammals into gardens has never been more vital.

Bats signal a healthy ecosystem

As the sun sets over our garden in summer, a small shadow flaps against the darkening sky while the hustle and bustle of city life continues. A tiny pipistrelle bat (*Pipistrellus pipistrellus*) flies low, looping around catching moths and mosquitoes before flying away to our neighbours' houses. A few minutes later and it's back, continuing its evening circuit, and everything feels good in the world.

What do bats eat?

Bats are insectivorous, picking insects off surfaces – such as spiders from plants and walls – or catching them in flight. A healthy population of moths is important for bats, especially night-flying moths, so growing plants that attract moths, such as the two pictured opposite, is one of the best things you can do for bats.

Their eyesight is good but they rely on echolocation to navigate and hunt in the dark, bouncing a continuous sequence of clicks off objects and insects. It's so accurate that they can detect the location of the smallest objects, including tiny flying insects as small as a midge. If you have bats in your garden it's a sign that you have a good ecosystem full of insects.

How to make homes for bats

Most bats rest, sleep and nest (roost) in trees such as oak and beech, favouring those in sunny, warm sites with good shelter. Many like to squeeze into cracks and crevices, especially when caring for their pups. Old trees with cavities or split wood caused by fallen or rotten branches are particular favourites.

If your garden is too small for such large trees, or you live in an urban area where town planners haven't planted enough, you can help by installing a bat box. These are adapted to bats' habits, with a slot at the bottom and a narrow crevice to sleep in, mimicking conditions in trees. In winter bats hibernate in warm places such as sheds, lofts and under the eaves of roofs.

Opposite, top Nathusius's pipistrelle bat, *Pipistrellus nathusii*.
Opposite, bottom left *Nicotiana alata* 'Lime Green'.
Opposite, bottom right Common honeysuckle, *Lonicera periclymenum*.

Recreate woodland edges to attract birds

Birds bring colour, drama and an audible beauty to our lives. I could watch and listen to the returning blackbirds, robins and great tits in our garden for hours, and when a new species appears, it's a moment of excitement. A number of birds nest in the trees and shrubs around our garden, and I find their dependence on the ecosystem I've helped to create the ultimate symbol of nature coming full circle. Birds, like bats, are a sign that your ecosystem is healthy.

According to Bird Life International, 40% of wild bird species are in decline, and one of the main reasons for garden-visiting species is loss of their preferred habitats and food in the wild. Many garden birds evolved along the fringes of woodlands, where trees meet scrub and grassland: a hub of habitat types offering lots of variety in food and shelter. Gardens unintentionally mirror this wild habitat because we put trees, shrubs and hedges around the boundaries, followed by lower perennials and annuals next to central lawns or patios. Most gardens are structured in this way, replicating woodland clearings or fringes, and you can help birds by going a step further. Bring birds into your garden ecosystem with these three essentials:

✛ **Shelter:** many garden birds evolved as woodland or scrub dwellers, and my top tip for attracting birds is to provide enough shelter for them to feel safe. If you have space, grow a mix of tall and medium-sized trees and shrubs, some evergreen and dense, others deciduous and open in form. Hedges and boundary shrubs are also excellent. Larger birds such as rooks and magpies tend to favour tall trees (10m/32ft or taller), while smaller birds such as tits and chaffinches prefer small trees and large shrubs (3–10m/10–32ft tall). If you only have a small garden like us, the larger trees will probably be nearby street trees or those in larger neighbouring gardens. In fact, we only have one small plum tree in our garden, but around the boundaries with our neighbours there are an additional seven trees of different types.

✛ **Water:** birds need fresh, clean water to drink, from a pond or bird bath. In our garden I favour a healthy wildlife pond (p.102) because it is self-cleaning, whereas a bird bath will need regular maintenance to avoid a build-up of bacteria and disease.

✛ **Food:** my preference is always for the garden ecosystem to provide enough food for its inhabitants naturally. For birds this starts with a healthy population of insects to eat, as well as worms. Aphids and caterpillars are very important during nesting season in spring and early summer, when the birds need lots of food near the nest to reduce flight distance and therefore energy expenditure. In winter, as well as insects, birds will eat seeds, fruit and berries, making plants that provide these essential in your garden.

Opposite, top Eurasian bullfinch, *Pyrrhula pyrrhula*. **Opposite, bottom** Goldfinch, *Carduelis carduelis*, on *Forsythia*.

Plants to attract birds

Attractive berry- or fruit-producing trees and shrubs

✝ *Crataegus monogyna* (hawthorn) – eventually forms a dense, spiky small tree that is good for nesting

✝ *Malus sylvestris* (crab apples) – trees can grow to a good size for birds to rest and nest in

✝ *Pyracantha* spp. – its sharp thorns make it a secure nesting spot for small birds

✝ *Rosa* spp. (just species that produce large hips, such as *R. canina*, *R. filipes* and *R. moyesii*)

✝ *Sambucus nigra*

✝ *Sorbus* spp. (rowan)

✝ *Viburnum opulus*

Plants for winter seeds

✝ *Dipsacus fullonum* (teasel)

✝ *Echinacea* spp.

✝ *Helianthus* spp. (sunflowers)

✝ *Knautia arvensis* (field scabious)

✝ *Verbena bonariensis*

Providing extra support for birds

Although I would prefer birds to be able to rely on natural sources for food and shelter, it can be useful to give them a helping hand.

✝ **Set up a bird feeder**: once you add a bird feeder, it's important to keep it stocked year-round and not stop, because birds will become reliant on it. Wash feeders regularly to reduce disease, and position them where squirrels can't reach them. Use black sunflower seeds, coarse oatmeal, soaked sultanas and, if you're not feeling squeamish, live mealworms and waxworms. Avoid peanuts, split peas and lentils, as these can cause problems for chicks.

✝ **Set up bird boxes**: in the absence of enough suitable habitat, such as shrubs, trees and even buildings (birds such as swifts, *Apus apus*, build mud nests under roof eaves), it can be helpful to add a bird box to your garden. Position it high enough up that cats and other predators can't reach it, and be sure to clean it out thoroughly in winter to reduce the chances of pests and diseases.

Make friends with mammals in the garden

Mammals are some of the shyest garden visitors and usually require a wider territory than our gardens can provide, with woodlands, hedgerows, grasslands and streams. But we can see our garden's ecosystem as part of that bigger one and set it up to help the mammals that move across it.

How to help mammals in the garden

Attract mammals to your garden by providing these three essentials.

Above Hedgehogs, *Erinaceus europaeus*, could become endangered in our lifetimes. They need all the habitat we can give them.

✝ **Access:** the greatest challenge to making our gardens accessible for mammals, such as hedgehogs, is walls and fences. Cutting out a small section of fence or having an area of hedge instead is a good solution (also helping birds), especially if your neighbours do the same, creating a mammal highway. Even in cities and towns, multiple gardens combined can make a large enough area for mammals to live happily.

✝ **Water:** drinking water is necessary for all wildlife, and by providing some in your garden you'll entice mammals in. An easily accessible pond with a gently sloping side for them to get in and out is ideal.

✝ **Shelter:** many mammals, such as badgers, shrews, rabbits and foxes, live in underground burrows or setts in soft, easy-to-dig soil and soil banks. Others, such as hedgehogs, want to snuggle into compost heaps and dry leaf litter under hedges and shrubs, so resist the temptation to tidy!

Five
Greening indoor space

I've always grown indoor plants, as unintentional mementos. A tall cactus, *Pilosocereus glaucescens*, that my grandparents gave me in 1999 as I left for university, destroyed in 2010 by Rumbles, has since regrown from a cutting. I'm looking at its towering shape as I type now, two decades later, thinking, 'Where has that time gone?'

Indoor plants stick by our sides. Physically the closest plants to us, they are one of the first things we see when we wake up; we breathe the same air. The fact that we invite plants into our homes is evidence to me that we need them around us to feel comfortable. We evolved waking up to plants.

They look pretty cool, too, lending our homes a daily dose of green, both calming and interesting whenever they sprout a new leaf or flower. Our care shapes how they grow, making each one unique to us, living treasures with a personal bond.

Green your work space

Research in hospitals has proved that live plants reduce stress and anxiety among patients, leading to an improved and shortened recovery. If plants can do that for people recuperating from illness or surgery, they must improve our daily wellbeing in our homes and workplaces. Studies around the world have shown that indoor plants dotted around the work space do indeed have this effect. Plants reduce physiological stress by making us feel more comfortable, reminding us of nature and providing an interesting, calming distraction from routine troubles.

Desk gardens

I spent fifteen years working in shared open-plan offices, and most of my week involved sitting at a small desk, staring at a computer screen and, quite often, a blank wall. For me, indoor plants played a crucial role in making those spaces bearable and even exciting – some days I'd rush to work to see if a new leaf had unfurled or if a flower had opened.

At my first office job I remember ordering three succulents to grow on my desk, including a ponytail palm (*Beaucarnea recurvata*), which sit next to my desk at home now, many years later, bonsaied through limited repotting. I've had plants growing on my desk in each job ever since and, now I work from home, the indoor jungle has grown.

I've found that not only do desk plants make the work space look more aesthetically pleasing and personal (especially in open-plan offices), but also they are essential to my wellbeing.

I enjoy this tiny, easy-to-care-for garden on my desk, bringing a little piece of nature indoors.

To grow houseplants on a desk, you will need to be fairly close to a window for sunlight. If your desk is in direct sun for most of the day you can easily grow cacti and succulents, which are perfectly suited to life indoors; houses and offices have dry climates most akin to arid deserts. Shadier desks can grow tropical plants that come from dark forest floors.

One desk plant is good, but I'd recommend growing a few, because you increase the chances of one of them doing something interesting at any given time of the year. On my desk *Rebutia* 'Apricot Ice' grows in spring and flowers in summer, while *Lithops salicola* grows new leaves in spring and flowers later in autumn.

Below *Asparagus densiflorus* 'Myersii', *Humata tyermanii*, *Araucaria heterophylla* and *Spathiphyllum wallisii* along with various smaller houseplants on the desk (see p.128).
Bottom Drought-tolerant plants are useful for roof terraces with little soil, such as *Verbena bonariensis*, *Phormium tenax* Purpureum Group and *Rosmarinus officinalis* Prostratus Group.

Meeting rooms

We spend a lot of time in meeting rooms, yet they can be empty, boring spaces that aren't at all conducive to collaboration and productive thought. Many are lucky to have windows. Occasionally a token palm will be added (*Chamaedorea elegans* is a good one), but I see meeting rooms as an opportunity to grow several large indoor plants together as a pot collection, exactly as plants in pots are arranged outside. With space for indoor trees and shrubs, carefully planned meeting rooms can house a sizable volume of greenery. In meeting rooms I've used *Strelitzia reginae*, the bird of paradise plant, with beautiful paddle leaves and striking orange flowers, and different species of large *Ficus* trees.

Office gardens

Office gardens and outdoor spaces, such as balconies, rooftop terraces and courtyards, are more important for our wellbeing at work than we give them credit for. As populations migrate to cities, these outdoor areas may be one of our few chances to see nature and make connections with the outside world. Adding plants is obviously a good thing for those physically using the spaces, but they are often seen from office windows too, making them doubly important.

Caring for indoor plants

Indoor life is warmer, drier and in most instances darker than outside. While houseplants behave in the same way as garden plants, they come from carefully selected habitats around the world that most closely match the indoor environment. As a result, there are some special rules to follow when caring for them.

Light

Most of the plants I grow are within 1m (3ft) of the window to receive the maximum light possible. This is because light levels indoors drop quickly further into the room, and won't sustain most plants. I've found the only plants I can grow with no direct sunlight at all are *Aspidistra* spp. and *Zamioculcas zamiifolia*, tucked around a corner from the window or a few metres into the room. Even these need some natural light. Most plants that thrive indoors are those from arid climates, such as cacti and succulents; these will need to be as close to a south-facing window as possible (north-facing in the southern hemisphere). It is now possible to supplement low light levels using LED grow lights, but natural light is always best.

Humidity

The most popular indoor plants are happy in the dry air of your home, but some leafier plants, such as *Calathea*, need a little more humidity to avoid crisped leaves. Misting is never a good option because the water soon evaporates and wetting leaves can trigger or exacerbate fungal infections. The best way to increase humidity indoors is to group plants together. Their combined mass and several pots of damp compost will create a microclimate with slightly increased humidity. For some plants that love humidity I will also add a saucer underneath the pot, fill it with 1cm (½in) of gravel or clay balls and keep it topped up with a little water.

Watering

As with plants outside, the amount of water indoor plants need varies. Cacti and succulents, such as *Opuntia microdasys* var. *albispina*, prefer to dry out completely between waterings, while some tropical plants, such as *Alocasia* x *amazonica* 'Polly', need constantly damp compost. The number one killer of indoor plants is overwatering, when the plants sit in wet compost and rot. I always wait until the surface of the compost is dry before watering anything, and never let a plant sit directly in water.

Feeding

I use diluted liquid seaweed fertiliser on all my indoor plants from spring to late summer, giving them a break in the colder autumn and winter months. Fast-growing tropical plants I fertilise weekly, slower plants like cacti and succulents monthly.

Opposite Front to back: Alocasia x amazonica 'Polly', Stromanthe sanguinea 'Triostar', Chamaedorea elegans and Ficus binnendijkii 'Amstel King'.
Right Tradescantia spathacea 'Tricolor', Tillandsia fuchsii, Tradescantia zebrina, Oxalis triangularis and Gynura aurantiaca.

Repotting

I repot indoor plants into a slightly bigger pot every two or three years using peat-free compost. Alternatively, I can use the same pot by root-pruning the plant, where I cut off the lower third of its roots and replant into new compost. This seems drastic, but is the same as looking after bonsai.

Create indoor plant combinations

Rather than grow plants randomly around our flat, I group them as I would plants outside, in a planned design to give extra impact.

Welcome to the indoor jungle

Turn part of your home into a dense, lush jungle by grouping a variety of leafy palms and smaller foliage plants.

Small tropicals

+ *Begonia* 'Black Knight', 'Connie Boswell', 'Pollux', 'Razzmatazz'
+ *Gynura aurantiaca*
+ *Humata tyermanii*
+ *Oxalis triangularis*
+ *Pilea peperomioides*
❶ *Sansevieria bacularis*
+ *Sansevieria trifasciata* 'Metallica'
+ *Tillandsia cyanea*
+ *Tradescantia spathacea* 'Tricolor'
+ *Tradescantia zebrina*

Medium-size tropicals

+ *Alocasia × amazonica* 'Polly'
+ *Asparagus densiflorus* 'Myersii'
+ *Aspidistra* spp.
+ *Calathea* 'Triostar'
+ *Cordyline fruticosa*
+ *Philodendron scandens*
+ *Philodendron* 'Xanadu'
+ *Stromanthe sanguinea* 'Triostar'
+ *Zamioculcas zamiifolia*

Large tropicals

+ *Beaucarnea recurvata*

+ *Chamaedorea elegans*
+ *Dracaena fragrans*
+ *Dracaena marginata*
+ *Ficus lyrata*
+ *Howea forsteriana*
+ *Philodendron pertusum*
+ *Strelitzia reginae*

Plant an indoor desert

A super-sunny window with more than 6 hours of direct sunlight per day is the perfect spot for a cactus and succulent collection. They have the most curious patterns and shapes, and often incredibly beautiful flowers. These slow-growing plants can be quite small and won't outgrow their spot anytime soon.

❷ *Aloe victoriae-reginae*
+ *Echinocactus* spp.
❸ *Euphorbia bupleurifolia* x *susannae*
❹ *Gymnocalycium* spp.
❺ *Kumara plicatilis*
❻ *Lithops salicola*
❼ *Opuntia microdasys* f. *albata*
+ *Pachyphytum oviferum*
+ *Pilosocereus glaucescens*
❽ *Rebutia* 'Apricot Ice'

Add some orchids

It came as a huge surprise to me that orchids are among the easiest plants to care for. I've always loved them, but had to suppress a growing obsession with them because I knew I'd get carried away and want to fill already crowded windowsills. Then one day I opened our front door to a friend thrusting a half-dead orchid at me and asking me to look after it while they went away for a couple of months. A standard moth orchid, *Phalaenopsis*, it only had leaves and some rotting roots, but over the course of those weeks I cared for it, trimming the damage, soaking the plant in water weekly and watching its silvery roots (which so many people cut off) turn green. Eventually a tendril grew from its centre, followed by buds that turned white and opened into flowers. I now have a small but growing collection and find they fit in well alongside any other houseplant, whether succulents or tropical. Orchids are among the hardest-working and most rewarding houseplants of all.

Mix everything up!

Of course, if you're feeling adventurous and you have a good measure of the conditions your houseplants need to grow well, mix them all up into a spectacular indoor combination. Who says you can't grow cacti, tropical and flowering plants together? One of the great things about indoor plants is that they're grown in pots and can be moved around.

The importance of pots

I grow all my houseplants in recycled or recyclable plastic pots or bamboo pots, sitting these within terracotta and glazed ornamental pots that also act as water reservoirs, protecting surfaces. In one room I have a display of all-white pots for a cleaner, more formal look, and in another room I mix up the colours but aim for earthy, natural-looking patterned pots. Plant pots can be as ornamental as the plants themselves, and the right combination makes a huge difference to the overall look. It's worth carefully curating your pots to match your plant combinations.

Cut flowers

I fell in love with cut flowers when I realised I could just chuck some in a vase and that was it. Nature's seasonal wonders could be brought inside to be observed and enjoyed up close, allowing me to appreciate every minute detail. Growing and picking your own cut flowers is particularly good for the planet, reducing CO2 emissions from transport; and when you're finished displaying them, pop them on to the compost heap.

Above Dahlia 'Nonette', 'Gitty Up' and an unnamed yellow variety I grew from seed. Alongside is foliage from cooking sage, *Salvia officinalis*, and flowers of the weed hoary mustard, *Hirschfeldia incana*, and faded *Achillea millefolium* 'Terracotta'.

What plants should I use?

Anything I think looks pretty is fair game – if it has scent, even better. As well as ornamental flowers I cut weeds, foliage, herbs, stems with berries, vegetables and even dried or dead flowers with structure for a long-lived display. I love simple glass vases, which let the plant stand out and allow me to see the stem, but use whatever you like most.

How to arrange cut flowers

I often like to have a single stem in a small vase to show off that one miraculous flower. When I do combine cut plants, I want a naturalistic look: light and airy arrangements with plenty of stem visible and space between everything. I try to capture some of the naturalistic combinations in the garden or the wild, such as the flowers *Daucus carota*, *Dahlia merckii* and *Persicaria amplexicaulis* 'September Spires' with foliage from *Eucalyptus pulverulenta* 'Baby Blue'. Playing with arrangements of cut flowers is a great way to experiment with new combinations for your garden in future years.

The best arrangements use a mix of complementary or contrasting colours, repetition, different shapes and sizes and foliage as a base. Colour is important; the bolder the flowers are and the more contrasting their colours, the more exciting and joyful the arrangement. Combinations with less contrast, using white and pastel-coloured flowers, are more relaxing.

In large vases it's helpful to place a supportive dome of chicken wire to poke stems through. Without this everything can flop to one side of the vase rather than staying where you'd like. Pin holders do a similar job: discs or squares with spikes that sit on the base of a vase for stems to be stuck into, looking neater in a transparent vase.

Tips for making cut flowers last

Some flowers last a long time once they've been cut (e.g. oxeye daisy), some don't (e.g. poppies) and some are in between (e.g. dahlias).

+ **Cut in early morning:** when flowers are freshest and full of sap.
+ **Make angled cuts:** this stops the stems sitting on the bottom of the vase, blocking water from getting in.
+ **Leave long stems:** I find flowers with reasonably long stems last longer because they hold more sap.

Six
Grow to nourish

One quiet afternoon alone on my allotment, lost in the thrum of buzzing bees, I rummaged around the raspberries. They tasted sweetest in that moment, warmed by the hazy summer sun.

How many millions of our ancestors have performed this simple action – picking and eating berries – since our time on earth began thousands of years ago? Yet in just the last century most of us have lost the chance to do this, our close relationship with the sources of our food severed by industrialisation, urbanisation and a barrage of plastic packaging.

In a world of eight billion people, we can't each grow enough food to feed ourselves. But growing a little opens a secret world of fruit and vegetable varieties not sold in shops, and every homegrown meal, even from small gardens or pots, reduces transport emissions and packaging sent to landfill.

My herbtopia

One very simple action anyone can take to help our planet is to grow herbs. Think of all those transport miles and plastic packets you can save. And herbs are among the easiest plants to keep alive with the right knowhow – ideal for serial plant murderers. It sounds too good to be true, but once established herbs provide a household with more than enough to snip for meals and drinks through most months of the year. For the rest, you can use dried or frozen stashes (see p.148).

Essential herbs to grow
Here I've listed my most essential, tried and tested herbs, and the conditions they need.

Full sun in free-draining soils

1 *Allium schoenoprasum* (chives) – leaves used in salads and cooking, with edible flowers – *perennial*

✢ *Artemisia dracunculus* (French tarragon) – for flavouring meals – *perennial*

2 *Foeniculum vulgare* 'Purpureum' (herb fennel) – leaves used with fish, seeds for snacking, flowers edible in salads – *perennial*

✢ *Laurus nobilis* (bay) – *perennial*

3 *Lavandula angustifolia* (English lavender) – I enjoy the edible flowers in ice cream and cocktails – *perennial*

✢ *Origanum majorana* (marjoram) – *perennial*

✢ *Origanum vulgare* (oregano) – *perennial*

4 *Salvia microphylla* – add flowers to cakes and cocktails – *perennial*

5 *Salvia officinalis* 'Purpurascens' (sage) – *perennial*

6 *Salvia rosmarinus* (rosemary) – makes a delicious simple syrup for cocktails and is used a lot in cooking; the edible flowers can be added to salads – *perennial*

✢ *Thymus serpyllum* (creeping thyme) – for cooking – *perennial*

7 *Thymus vulgaris* (cooking thyme) – *perennial*

Full sun in fertile, moisture-retentive soils

✢ *Borago officinalis* (borage) – has white or blue, cucumber-flavoured edible flowers – *perennial*

✢ *Matricaria chamomilla* (chamomile) – edible flowers most commonly used for making tea, but can also be used to flavour cream and ice cream – *annual*

✢ *Monarda didyma* (bergamot) – Earl Grey-esque tea and edible flowers – *perennial*

8 *Ocimum basilicum* (basil, purple and green) – for pesto, salads and in cooking – *annual*

✛ *Perilla frutescens* var. *crispa* (bicolor and red types) – for salads – *annual*

✛ *Tagetes lemmonii* (Mexican marigold) – makes tea for sore stomachs – *perennial*

Full sun indoors

✛ *Cymbopogon citratus* (lemon grass) – used to flavour rice, curries, chicken dishes and many other meals, as well as in cocktails and tea infusions – *perennial*

9 *Persicaria odorata* (Vietnamese coriander) – add to stir fries, chopped to flavour dishes in the same way as regular coriander, and in salads – *perennial*

Part-shade in fertile, moisture-retentive soils

✛ *Anethum graveolens* (dill) – beautiful with fish – *annual*

✛ *Angelica gigas* – use leaves in salads, and two-year-old stems can be candied *biennial/perennial*

✛ *Melissa officinalis* (lemon balm) – for tea – *perennial*

10 *Mentha spicata* (spearmint) – for tea, sauces, mojitos! – *perennial*

11 *Mentha suaveolens* 'Variegata' (pineapple mint)

✛ *Myrrhis odorata* (sweet cicely) – improves rhubarb flavour – *perennial*

12 *Petroselinum crispum* 'Italian Giant' (flat-leaved parsley) – chopped as a garnish for hot meals and salads – *annual*

✛ *Rumex sanguineus* (red-veined sorrel) – adds a citrus tang to salads – *perennial*

Herbs in the house

✛ Indoor growing won't suit many herbs long-term because even for those from warm climates our homes can be too dry, and even sunny windowsills aren't as bright as being outdoors. But annuals such as basil can be grown year-round in a sunny window, using a grow light in winter months, as can the tender herbs lemon grass, Vietnamese coriander and ginger. Extend fresh basil and coriander into winter by sowing in pots outside in late summer to bring into the kitchen in early autumn.

Opposite, clockwise from top left Origanum 'Kent Beauty' (ornamental), Salvia rosmarinus 'Albus' and Borago officinalis 'Alba'.

Designer herbs for contemporary gardens

I've always been attracted to the look of herb plants, their soft, pale leaves, structured form and subtle flowers that seem to glow in yellows, whites, blues and purples. I can't think of a single ugly herb and I use them in almost every garden I design.

Memories of warmer climes

A trip to Malibu, California, really sparked my exploration of using edible herbs ornamentally. I noticed prostrate rosemary (*Salvia rosmarinus* Prostrata Group) in flower, trailing over a modern wall. The stems hung vertically against a horizontal pattern in cast concrete, simple and smart.

Many herbs, including rosemary, sage and some thymes, originated in warm, dry climates and have evolved soft, light-green to silvery, sun-reflecting foliage; they also form neat wind-resistant, mounded hummocks to help them survive harsh summers. Using herb foliage in garden designs brings light, gentle hues into the colour scheme which make it soft and inviting, while the plant forms – like comforting cushions – give a relaxed, informal feel.

Structural herbs

I'll often use rosemary and sage as structural plants in a design, for smaller or airier plants to dance around. Both come in a variety of cultivars with differing taste and appearance: *Salvia rosmarinus* 'Barbecue' is a particularly rigid vertical, while *S. officinalis* 'Purpurascens' and 'Purpurascens Variegata' are both useful alternative sages. Bay clipped to size is another solid evergreen edible shrub when a darker shade is needed.

Herbal hedges

Prostrate rosemary is useful for clipping into a dense, low hedge 30–50cm (12–20in) tall, and regular rosemary can be grown into a larger hedge of up to 1.5m (5ft). Bay wants to become a huge tree but takes heavy pruning well and can be maintained as a tall evergreen hedge of 2m (6½ft) or more. For something less formal, lavender (*Lavandula angustifolia*) has long been used as a low hedge, and sage can be grown as an informal hedge up to 1m (3ft) tall.

Ground-covering and trailing herbs

I've already mentioned the excellent prostrate rosemary, and another herb I

Opposite *Salvia officinalis* sits in an ornamental planting with *Pennisetum* 'Hameln' and the dried seed heads of *Astrantia major* subsp. *involucrata* 'Shaggy'.

regularly use for ground cover is the short *Thymus serpyllum*, which slowly creates a cushiony blanket with flowers in white, pink or purple in early summer loved by pollinators. Oregano spreads in a similar way and I grow the attractive *Oreganum* 'Kent Beauty'. Miniature Corsican mint (*Mentha requienii*) can be grown in part-shade for eating, though its small leaves are fiddly to pick.

Temporary crowd-pleasers

Purple basil (*Ocimum basilicum* var. *purpurascens*) is one of the more beautiful foliage herbs and often has light pink flowers too. It can be grown from seed and planted out around the garden in summer (try 'Red Rubin' or 'Purple Ruffles'). Less well known is annual *Perilla frutescens*, used regularly in Asian cuisine and available with deep purple, green or bicoloured leaves. The leaves look pretty and taste fresh in salads.

Punctuation herbs

Various herbs can be used as punctuation points to pause on when looking at plantings. Herbs such as fennel and dill (*Anethum graveolens*) have light, lacy leaves to reduce transpiration (water evaporating from leaf pores), adding to their appearance an airiness usually reserved for grasses. I plant fennel – either regular green or bronze-tinged *Foeniculum vulgare* 'Purpureum' – in almost every garden and let it run riot in my planting schemes. Gradually growing tall, its fluffy leaves between other plants soften the overall look and mingle well with other flowers, and it has wonderful flat yellow umbels.

Chives (*Allium schoenoprasum*) are low-growing but incredibly useful for their grassy leaves and purple flowers as mini vertical focal points in tricky corners, even in some shade. *Angelica archangelica* (pale green flowers) and *A. gigas* (dark purple flowers) create eye-catching plants with their statuesque form.

Fennel, dill, angelica and chives self-seed readily; you simply remove the plants you don't want. In drier climates fennel can get out of control.

Designer herbs in pots

Natural toughness and drought tolerance make most herbs well adapted to sunny, exposed locations, including roof terraces, raised beds and even large pots. Chives look lovely in window boxes.

In shadier spots, mint is excellent in large pots (20cm/8in and wider) and window boxes. Mint comes in a wide variety of flavours and looks to match: *Mentha suaveolens* 'Variegata' has white-variegated leaves and *M. longifolia* Buddleia Mint Group particularly long mauve flowers.

Herbs for wellness

Unique in the garden for their multisensory properties, herbs benefit both mind and body. Besides the nutrients they provide and their use in healing, through their aromas herbs jog our memories and provoke our dreams. I'll often stand in the middle of my herb bed, soaking up their fragrance as their oils are released by the warmth of the sun, feeling better for it.

Healing with herbs

Sometimes the act of weeding my herb bed helps calm my mind. Sweet and musky scents overpower my senses and knock any worries out of the way as fond memories are brought to the fore. It is scent that connects me most to the natural world around me.

In the past, people took plants and their relationship to wellbeing more seriously, relying on herbs for many treatments as medicines, poultices and more. Today we have modern medicine for most ailments but have generally forgotten that for simple things – soothing a sore throat, gaining a natural nutrient boost, calming our nerves – herbs have a role.

Scientists at London's Kew Gardens have found that German chamomile (*Matricaria chamomilla*), used for tea, has anti-inflammatory, antispasmodic and antiseptic properties. A carbohydrate in *Echinacea purpurea* roots has been found in clinical studies to stimulate the nervous system and produce a reduction in cold symptoms. A substance derived from yew trees (*Taxus baccata*),

Above Many herbs can be steeped in boiling water for a few minutes for healthy teas – this is mint.

poisonous if eaten, is now used in cancer treatments around the world.

There is a great deal we still don't know about plant properties, which makes the destruction of our natural world all the more tragic – we're wiping out species before we have a chance to know or understand them.

Calming herbs

I often feel on edge and anxious, and have found that warm teas help my body relax naturally. Tea made from German chamomile in particular calms me down before I try to get to sleep. Leave a few teaspoons of dried flower heads to steep in boiling water for 5–10 minutes.

Herbs for sore throats

Peppermint (*Mentha* x *piperita*) tea will soothe a sore throat or tickly cough, while adding fresh ginger (*Zingiber officinale*) – which can be grown as a houseplant – to kale smoothies or to lemon and honey tea helps to soothe and contains mild antiseptics. German chamomile tea's anti-inflammatory and antiseptic properties also help to alleviate sore throats.

Herbs for upset stomachs

Lemon balm (*Melissa officinalis*) drunk as a tea contains a slight sedative useful to soothe mild stomach upsets and to aid sleep. Chewing fresh green fennel seeds with their sweet aniseed flavour helps settle my stomach, as does peppermint tea, a widely drunk post-dinner nightcap.

Nutritious herbs

Parsley (*Petroselinum crispum*) and basil (*Ocimum basilicum*) are very rich in vitamins A and C, and thyme (*Thymus vulgaris*) is rich in vitamin C. All herbs contain various vitamins, minerals and nutrients that are good for the body when added to our meals, so using a mix of herbs increases the benefit.

Powerful scented herbs

Lavender has sedative properties and many people report that the smell alone makes them feel sleepy. The sweet scent of *Salvia microphylla* 'Nachtvlinder' and *Monarda didyma* 'Cambridge Scarlet' with its bergamot Earl Grey tea scent I find addictive. I'll often brush rosemary and thyme plants with my hand to release their soothing and evocative fragrance.

Habitats for happy herbs

Even if you've had a bad experience growing herbs in the past, I promise you'll have better luck by understanding the plant, how it wants to grow and where it grows naturally.

Annual or perennial?

Most culinary herbs fall into the perennial category and keep growing year after year, making them great value. They include rosemary, fennel, sage, thyme, oregano, chives and lavender. Some other favourites, such as basil, dill, coriander (*Coriandrum sativum*) and chamomile, are annuals, which means they grow for one year before dying (biennials last for two, e.g. parsley). Chamomile, coriander and parsley will self-sow naturally if some flower heads are left on, while basil seeds are sown each year fresh.

Sun versus shade

The majority of herbs love full, blasting-hot direct sunshine all day long. Only a few like partial shade, such as mint, sweet cicely (*Myrrhis odorata*), chives and lemon balm, but even these do best with a few hours of direct sun.

Opposite Plants that love full sun and dry conditions make great 'plant and forget' street plantings, here Salvia rosmarinus, Lavandula angustifolia, Perovskia atriplicifolia, Buddleia davidii and Cortaderia selloana.

Soil fertility and drainage

Sun lovers, such as rosemary, thyme, sage and lavender, are from Mediterranean regions where summers are dry and the soil is poor and free-draining, so it is best to recreate these conditions as best you can. Growing these plants in sandy or gritty soil in raised beds or in pots works well. Alternatively, add lots of horticultural grit (special lime-free, small, washed grit) to the planting holes for extra drainage. I find those that like a bit of shade, as well as fennel, dill and angelica, enjoy richer soils and slightly more moisture in summer.

Size

The small pots of herbs we buy in shops are misleading, because most herbs want to become large plants! For better sustainability and as a source of herbs to eat, the bigger the better it is for you too; having armfuls of herbs at your disposal means you never have to scrimp on flavour. Don't cram rosemary and sage into a small space or pot together, as each will quickly form a shrub 1m (3ft) or more in size. You can clip them to keep them in check as you harvest leaves to eat.

Harvest, use and store herbs

Nothing beats cooking with fresh herbs that you've grown yourself. And in some instances you can lengthen their lifespan by drying them for a more intense flavour. Here are my rules for making the most of herbs and minimising their waste.

Fresh herbs and how to use them

A rule of thumb for most herbs is to pick the younger shoots, keeping enough leaves lower down the stems so the plant can build energy from sunlight to regrow. Never take more than a third of the plant at one time, chives being an exception – you can snip all of those and they'll regrow.

Most herbs can be stored in the fridge for a few days, but by growing them you shouldn't ever need to do this in the growing season. All herbs can be frozen in sealed bags or containers to keep them fresh for winter use. Containers are available that can be attached to a grinder, so you can mill the frozen herbs into your cooking.

Drying herbs is a little more involved but is the main way of storing them, and means you can keep them ready to use in a cupboard for most of the year (exactly like the herbs you'd buy in shops). Combine dried herbs into your own preferred mixes.

Above Herbs can be dried very easily by tying them up in bunches and hanging them upside down in a dry cupboard.

Above One easy use for herbs is to flavour shop-bought olive oil. Add the herb or mix of herbs of your choice to the bottle of oil and leave for the flavours to infuse for two weeks, then strain and use the oil within two months. To create flavoured chilli oil, heat the oil and fresh or dried chillies for a few minutes, remove and allow to cool, then add to a sterilised jar.

How to dry-store herbs

✛ Pick herb stems 15–20cm (6–8in) long, as many as you may need.

✛ Tie the stems gently together into bundles with a piece of twine or cotton and hang them upside down somewhere dry and dark, such as a cupboard.

✛ Leave for approximately ten days, until fully dried and crispy.

✛ You can cover the bundles with muslin or a loose paper bag to keep out dust and catch falling seeds or leaves (don't use plastic, as this traps moisture).

✛ Flowers, such as chamomile, are best dried out flat on a tray for the same amount of time, and stored when ready.

✛ Store dried herbs separately in airtight containers in a cool, dark cupboard. Keep leaves whole for more flavour, or remove any stems and crush using a rolling pin.

✛ Don't forget to label the jars, as dried herbs all look the same!

Grow your own vegetables

I have hazy childhood memories of sowing beginner edibles such as spring onion and radish, next to ripe strawberries and gooseberries, then shelling fresh peas into a metal colander. As an adult I returned to growing vegetables in pots on our patio, and then in a tiny raised bed in our local community garden. Despite the inner-city location, I produced bagfuls of veg, often supervised by a robin.

Top tips for veg success

Vegetables are high-maintenance plants. They need regular attention, watering, tying in, fertilising and protecting from pests for the best results. Growing your own edibles can also sometimes cost the same or more than buying mass-produced stuff in the shops. Don't let this put you off, because you will have good results and the freshest possible food. However, I've learned over the years that it helps to target my efforts.

Know your limitations

Originally, I wanted to be as self-sufficient as possible when it came to vegetables. Although my allotment is large enough to do this and I now know I'm capable of achieving it with some edibles, I quickly found I didn't have the time or energy outside my full-time job to mollycoddle the plants. It's still an aim for the future to produce most of our own veg, but for now I remain content if I grow enough for two or three meals a week, even if it's only one portion each time. The same is true if you're limited by space; grow what you can as efficiently as possible, knowing infrequent harvests are still a success.

Allow time for harvesting

Harvesting takes a surprisingly long time, something I hadn't accounted for. On the whole I manage to spend about two hours per week on my plot (perhaps double that in the height of hot summers to water). From mid-summer to autumn on a reasonably sized plot, harvesting vegetables can take up all of that time, leaving less time for weeding.

Prioritise sowing crops

Weeding and tidying is always last on my to do list. It is important, as weeds can compete with the veg, yet rarely as much as we're told. I always prioritise sowing more seeds over weeding to keep the plot full, which in itself reduces space for weeds. While my plot never looks the neatest, it does have high yields. Adding a 3cm-deep (1–2in) mulch of peat-free compost or well-rotted manure, rather than digging it in when preparing your veg beds, will also help reduce weeds.

Focus on yield

Speaking of which, try to choose crops that have a high yield-to-effort ratio. French beans, tomatoes, chard and kale can be picked over a number of weeks and even months, making them high-value plants compared to the effort you put in. Cabbages, on the other hand, are a one-hit wonder – I rarely bother with them.

Sow successive crops

With many vegetables that don't repeat crop, it's best to sow little and often for a constant supply, so that as one batch hits the plate, another is sown or planted out. Salad and quick-to-ripen crops like radish, spring onion, beetroot, turnip, mustards, mibuna and kohlrabi can be ready to eat in a matter of weeks, so I sow them monthly from spring until the end of summer. Slower crops like peas, beans and carrots are worth sowing three or four times across spring–summer too.

Go organic

Gardening organically saves time because a healthy ecosystem leads to healthier, bug- and disease-resistant plants (beneficial insects do half of my pest control for me; see p.105). Choose seeds that are resistant to bugs and diseases to start things off on the right foot.

Above Sweetcorn 'Damaun', potatoes 'Charlotte' and 'Anya', white onions and carrot 'Resistafly'.

Be efficient with space

You don't need a huge plot to produce lots of vegetables. If you have only a few metres of soil, or a handful of 40cm (16in) pots, squeeze loads of produce out by tying the above principles together and dividing the area into:

✚ High-yield plants – grow vine tomatoes and French beans up canes for repeat yields in little space.

✚ Successive sowing – split another area into three or four squares (or pots) and sow fast-growing salad crops into one each month for a conveyor belt of food.

✚ Small crops – small, fast-growing crops, such as radish and beetroot, can also be snuck in around other plants or in gaps.

Grow with the seasons

In order to grow the most vegetables, it's important to think seasonally, which means having something to harvest in every month of the year. Variety in seasonal produce connects us to nature's calendar and makes mealtimes more exciting.

Plan for crops in every season

Growing seasonally is slightly complicated because all vegetables grow at different speeds and times: a radish in summer can grow in about a month, but if you want to pick Brussels sprouts in winter it could take almost a year for them to be ready. In time and with practice, scheduling for this becomes second nature and very rewarding. I find it helps to keep things simple by splitting the year into two main growing seasons.

Autumn and winter

Hardy salad crops sown in early autumn under the cover of fleece or in a greenhouse or polytunnel can be picked throughout winter. Autumn is also time for final sowings of overwintering peas, broad beans and garlic, ready to eat early the following year.

Think like a squirrel by harvesting, prepping and storing food in autumn to tide you over through winter. Squash, pumpkins, beans and pulses grown in summer should be stored in a cool, dark place. Some vegetables can be parboiled and frozen, including runner beans and peas.

Hardier crops such as kale, Brussels sprouts, chard, parsnips, carrots and leeks that were sown in spring and summer can be left out in the garden and harvested as and when needed.

Spring and summer

The main sowing period is in spring, when warmer weather and longer days send happy plants rocketing. Most plants can be sown in spring, including tomatoes, potatoes, squash and courgettes.

Don't start too early, though; sow when soil is over 5°C/41°F (check online or measure with a thermometer), between mid- and late spring. In early spring seedlings are likely to stop growing, sulking in the cold and rotting. The exceptions are chillies and aubergines; they take such a long time to grow, they must be sown indoors in late winter to give them a head start.

Summer is when you sow small amounts of certain fast-growing crops every few weeks for a constant supply, such as lettuce, radish and beetroot.

Opposite Squash 'Disco' (plain white) is best eaten fresh, while 'Sweet Dumpling' (with green stripes) can be stored through winter.

Save seeds for next year

I'd always felt that collecting the seeds of vegetables I'd grown, rather than relying on bought seed packets, was for some reason, well, a little bit naughty, not to mention complicated, requiring a qualification in plant wizardry. But slowly and surely I became a rebel and found that saving homegrown seeds is not only easy, it saves money and is rewarding, fun and empowering.

Why collect your own vegetable seeds?

Storing seeds will cut down on packaging and transportation, and you'll know they are raised without potentially harmful chemicals. Better yet, because each generation of plants exhibits some variations, such as stronger disease resistance or different colours, you can select your favourites for the following year and gradually improve what you grow.

To avoid mixing up varieties of the same plant (e.g. red and green lettuce), only grow one at a time, or make sure you grow them far away from each other to avoid cross-pollination – unless you want to try crossbreeding! Squash, pumpkin and cucumbers (the cucurbits) should never be crossbred, as this can introduce qualities that cause upset stomachs. Be sure to remove the plants with undesirable traits (e.g. weak growth compared to neighbours) before they flower to stop this being passed into next year.

Bear in mind that you shouldn't save seeds from some vegetables where the results can be variable. Named varieties with 'F1' in the name come from very particular breeding programmes, and their seedlings won't look the same as the parent. Despite this, there are many that will come true, and it's always worth experimenting to see what happens.

Vegetable seeds to collect
+ lettuce
+ peas
+ beans (runner, French and broad)
+ onions and leeks
+ radishes
+ tomatoes
+ carrots and parsnips
+ brassicas (cabbage, Brussels sprout, kale, broccoli, kohlrabi)
+ beetroot and chard
+ cucurbits (pumpkins, squash and courgettes)
+ garlic (use the cloves, not the seeds)

Above When dried, seed pods like Pea 'Blackdown Blue' are easily prised open. If the seed heads are still green, the seed won't be ready.

How to collect and store your own vegetable seeds

1 Seeds are generally ready when the flower heads or seed pods are browned, dry and starting to open – keep an eye on plants to catch them before the seeds fall naturally. Carefully remove the seeds or knock them into a bag. Use a paper bag or envelope to prevent moisture build-up (avoid plastic bags for this reason).

2 With plants like radish, lettuce and brassicas, where the seed develops in large inflorescences (flower clusters), you may prefer to cut the plant at the base as the seed starts turning brown, but before it is ripe. Hang it upside down indoors with the bag tied over the flowers to catch falling seeds.

3 For tomatoes and cucurbits, scoop the seeds out, rinse in a sieve to remove the flesh, and leave them to dry on a plate for a few days before storing.

4 Peas and beans are best picked just before the pods are fully dry and split open. Leave the pods in a tray on a windowsill until they split and the seeds can be removed.

5 Write the full name of the plant and the date on the paper bag or envelope. In six months' time it will be impossible to remember what the seeds are otherwise!

6 Store in a cold, dry and dark place until you are ready to sow.

Hearty and wholesome

Robust vegetables that fill me up and are packed with nutrition are first on my annual list of crops to grow on my allotment. I find most of these plants are tough, and only require low levels of maintenance once established. Here are some of my absolute favourites for flavour and vigour, after trialling hundreds of varieties.

Alliums
- Garlic (from cloves): 'Germidour', 'Printanor', 'Messidrome' – all soft-neck types for long storage.
- Leeks: 'Bandit', 'Northern Lights'.
- Onions: brown 'Ailsa Craig' and red 'Carmen' from seed.

Brassicas
- Broccoli: 'Early Purple Sprouting'.
- Brussels sprouts: 'Brenden' and, for fun, purple 'Rubine'.
- Kale: 'Red Devil', 'Red Russian' (1), 'Nero di Tuscano', 'Fizz' (2)– all have smooth leaves, reducing hiding places for whitefly.
- Kohlrabi: purple and white.
- Pak choi: add leaves to salads. (3)

Cucurbits
- Courgette: 'Black Beauty', 'Romanesco', 'Eight Ball'.
- Pumpkin: 'White Ghost' for extra Halloween spookiness and flavour.
- Summer squash: 'Jaune et Vert', 'Disco'.
- Winter squash: 'Honey Bear', 'Musquée de Provence', 'Sweet Dumpling', 'Crown Prince'.

Fabaceae
- French beans: 'Cobra' for volume, 'Borlotti Firetongue' for drying.
- Broad beans: 'Super Aguadulce' for overwintering and summer.
- Mangetout: 'Reuzensuiker', 'Golden Sweet', 'Shiraz'.
- Pea: 'Meteor' for autumn sowing, 'Blackdown Blue' and 'Jumbo' for sowing through summer.

Perennials
- Asparagus: 'Vittorio', 'Backlim', 'Pacific Purple'.
- Globe artichokes: 'Violetta', 'Green Globe' – easy to cook and best eaten young.
- Jerusalem artichokes – toughest veg on the plot.

Roots
- Carrot: 'Resistafly', 'Purple Sun' – both taste sweet.
- Main crop potatoes: 'British Queen' and 'Mayan Gold' for roasts and chips.
- New potatoes: 'Pink Fir Apple' and 'Charlotte' for flavour.
- Parsnip: 'Gladiator' – enormous and delicious.
- Salsify: for adding a slightly oyster flavour when roasted or puréed.

Other
- Celeriac: 'Monarch', 'Ibis' – makes a delicious coleslaw.
- Chard: 'Rhubarb' – an easy-growing green, best stir-fried.
- Mooli radish: fantastic in salads and stir-fries.

Top Cauliflower 'Graffiti'.
Above Broccoli 'Early Purple Sprouting'.

Fresh and flavoursome

Salad crops are my favourites to grow because they give such a swift return. With extremely fast results – many grow in just a month or so – you can present friends and family with impossibly fresh dishes of homegrown goodness throughout the summer. Though many salad crops are limited to growing in the warmest months, giving others – such as lettuces or mustard – a little protection using a greenhouse, polytunnel or horticultural fleece means winter can be just as productive, and delicious!

Salads

- Amaranth 'Garnet Red' (4) – add young leaves to salads.
- Beetroot: 'Boltardy'.
- Florence fennel: 'Mantovano'.
- Lettuce: 'Bugatti' (5), 'Forellenschluss', 'Red little Gem' (6) 'Salad Bowl' (7) – grow 'cut and come again' types whose leaves will regrow for a couple of months.
- Mibuna (8).
- Mizuna: 'Red Baron' (13).
- Mustard: 'Frizzy Lizzy' or 'Red Frills' (9), with a purple hue and a good mustard flavour.
- Mustard spinach: *Brassica rapa* var. *perviridis*.

- Nasturtium: 'Alaska' (10) – the attractive marbled leaves have a milder flavour in young plants.
- Pak choi: add leaves to salads.
- Radish: 'French Breakfast 3'.
- Red-veined sorrel (11).
- Rocket.
- Spinach (perpetual) (12).

Solanaceae

- Aubergine: 'Pot Black', 'Pin Stripe' – prolific miniature varieties for pots and patios.
- Tomatoes: 'Green Zebra', 'Sun Gold', 'Artisan Mix' grown as vines, or 'Vilma' as a small bush.

Edible flowers

Colour brings excitement to meals, and often the plants can be grown in pots by the door and in window boxes, making them cheery edibles accessible to all. Another benefit of edible flowers is that before they're picked, they'll be used by pollinators, so will feed you and the local wildlife.

My essential edible flowers

✤ *Allium ursinum* (wild garlic) – add the garlicky flowers to salads or use to garnish soups.

✤ *Anethum graveolens* (dill) – use as a garnish, as you would the leaves.

❶ *Borago officinalis* (borage), classic blue or white varieties – use the cucumber-flavoured flowers on salads or to garnish a G&T.

❷ *Calendula officinalis* Touch of Red Series or classic yellow and orange – pluck the slightly peppery petals to sprinkle on salads.

❸ *Centaurea cyanus* 'Black Ball' or classic blue cornflower – add to salads.

✤ Hibiscus – petals are edible in salads or dried for teas.

✤ Lavender (any) – use whole flowers to give cocktails a Parma violet taste, or sprinkle petals into salads or over ice cream.

❹ *Monarda didyma* – with a slight Earl Grey flavour and perfect for decorating cakes and desserts or in salads.

❺ *Nasturtium* 'Alaska' – add to salads for some spice.

❻ *Pelargonium* 'Attar of Roses' – tastes subtly of Parma violet, the leaves even more so.

✤ *Pisum sativum* (peas) – add the showy flowers to salads – but you'll sacrifice a pod each time.

✤ Rose petals – decorate cakes or add to boiling water and strain for tea.

❼ *Salvia microphylla* 'Cerro Potosí' and 'Nachtvlinder' are good, but any will do – slightly sweet, great sprinkled on cakes, ice cream and other desserts or added to salad.

❽ *Viola* (any) – perfect on desserts, cakes and salads.

Opposite Edible flowers make fun and colourful additions to meals, drinks, desserts and cakes.

Grow your own fruit

On my allotment I grow a number of small apple trees that provide delicious fruit every year without fail. Doing this opened my eyes to the trees lining our road at home. I had ignored them for years, but I learned that they're unusual not only because they grow large edible fruit, but because they're the little-known Nashi pear from Asia (*Pyrus pyrifolia*). They taste gritty and sweet like a pear, along with melon and strawberries combined. An autumn highlight I look forward to, leaving me wondering why every street isn't an orchard of free food.

Grow fruit trees

You don't need an orchard to grow apples, pears and cherries. Many fruit trees can be grown in the tiniest of spaces with savvy training and pruning, or you can grow varieties on special dwarfing rootstocks that keep them small. Cultivars are all grown from cuttings, making them exact clones of the parent plant, growing exactly the right fruit. However, these cuttings can be grafted on to roots of other varieties, allowing us to choose how large they grow. Apple root stocks range from M27 and M9, stopping at head height, up to taller M26 and M106, or the fully grown M25. Dwarf pears are grown on Quince C rootstock, comparable in size to M27 for apples.

With their beautiful fruits through the summer and autumn, and insect-friendly blossoms in spring, mini fruit trees are great additions to any garden. It's the pruning that I find enjoyable, losing myself in the process, a true collaboration between me and the plant.

Above Apple 'Katy' collected and ready to be eaten.
Opposite Apple 'Pinova' trained as a stepover, showing that even small spaces can have abundant fruit crops.

How to grow mini fruit trees

I've trained knee-high (45cm/18in) apple trees into T shapes on my allotment; with two horizontal branches, they're called 'stepover trees' because, well, you can. Look for M27 rootstock for the smallest trees, which are suitable for growing in large pots, trained or as normal-shaped mini trees. I grow 'Pinova', 'Katy' and 'Falstaff', but seek advice from a local grower about those that do well in your area. Pears can be grown in this way on the rootstock Quince C.

In sunny, warm spots I grow figs, restrained within large pots or stone slabs buried in the ground. Restricting their roots keeps them small and improves fruiting. I grow 'Brown Turkey', purple 'Rouge de Bordeaux' and striped 'Panachée'; 'Dorée' is also good in pots.

Fruit trees grown in the ground require very little maintenance besides pruning. With no need to water or fertilise them once they're established, they give back more to us and the environment than they take.

Quick guide to pruning apples and pears

✛ **Summer pruning:** in late summer, snip all side shoots over 20cm (8in) back to the third leaf joint above the cluster of leaves at the base of the shoot, to keep its size and vigour in check. These side shoots are known as spurs, and it's these that flower and develop fruit. Remove vigorous upright growth completely.

✛ **Winter pruning:** remove dead, damaged, rubbing or diseased stems completely. If the main branches have grown, cut them back by a third to concentrate the plant's energy into a smaller area. Remove any vigorous upward-growing shoots at the centre of the tree completely, otherwise they will want to become the leading trunk.

How to grow berries

Expensive to buy in shops but relatively easy to grow, berries are your wallet's friend. Most berry plants crop year after year with hardly any effort on your part. As much as I love and encourage birds, they'll want to eat berries more than you. Protect your produce with netting, horticultural fleece or purpose-built cages, but check daily because birds can sometimes get caught in them. Plant berry-producing shrubs specifically for birds, to keep them happy too (see pp.119–20 on birds).

Raspberries

When growing fruit, it's best to focus on what you like. We love raspberries and they're straightforward to grow, so for us they were an easy choice.

Raspberries are available in two types: summer-fruiting, which crop earlier all in one go, and autumn-fruiting, which crop slowly from late summer into early autumn. If you have space, grow a mix of the two types and allow 6–8 stems (called canes) per plant.

Summer-fruiting types, while delicious, I find require more work because fruit appears on two-year-old stems that need a support structure. Because they fruit all at once you end up with excess amounts, useful for jam or freezing, but I rarely have time for this. I cut corners by only growing the autumn-fruiting 'Joan J' and 'Polka', which crop slowly enough for picking over a couple of months (yellow 'All Gold' are also recommended). These don't really need support, but if you're on an exposed spot, they can benefit from being grown against a fence and tied

Above Autumn raspberry 'Joan J'

with twine into horizontal wires set at 0.6m (2ft), 1.2m (4ft) and 1.8m (6ft) from the ground. Or run the wires between freestanding strong posts.

Normally with autumn raspberries you cut all the stems down to the ground in winter, and new shoots will grow again in spring. By leaving a stem or two per plant over winter, you'll find they fruit again in small amounts in early summer the next year, like the summer-fruiting types. Don't overdo this, though, or the fresh autumn crop can suffer.

Blackberries

Blackberries are fearsome, spiky things, but, the fruit when warmed in the sun is exquisite. My allotment perimeter is lined with them, growing like weeds that everyone forages from. To grow your own, treat them like raspberries but restrict the number of growing stems to four per plant and tie them in a fan shape against a fence or wall, or on wires. Allow four new stems to grow in the summer, and tie them together in the middle while the previous years' flower and fruit fan out to the sides. Once fruiting finishes, cut the old stems off at the base and spread the new stems out ready to repeat next year.

Strawberries

A small patch or pot of strawberries is always worthwhile, replanted every few years from the offshoots (called runners) that turn into vigorous new plants. It's worth slipping some ink-free card underneath the fruit as they form to protect them from mud and mould.

Gooseberries

I never expected to be keen on gooseberries, but they converted me when I discovered sweet 'Hinnonmaki Red' and 'Hinnonmaki Yellow'. They are extremely easy to grow and easier to eat in a gooseberry fool or sliced on tarts. Gooseberry bushes are vigorous and need little care, but it's beneficial to prune using secateurs in winter, while they are dormant keeping only four or five main branches to form an open goblet shape, from which smaller side branches grow and fruit. They are spiky, so remember to wear thick gloves.

Blueberries

If you don't have acidic soil, blueberries are worth growing in a 30cm (12in) wide pot filled with acidic (ericaceous) peat-free compost. 'Duke' is a reliable cultivar. Position in a sunny spot. On plants over two years old, cut a quarter of the main stems off at the base in late winter to encourage vigorous new shoots.

Something exotic

For something a bit different, look to Chilean guava (*Ugni molinae*), with fruit tasting of boiled sweets, and the hardy kiwi vine, *Actinidia deliciosa*. 'Jenny' doesn't need a partner plant to be fertilised, as other kiwis usually do. Both do need full sun, in which they'll grow and crop happily year after year.

Seven
The world is your garden

Growing up in the countryside, my siblings and I ran amok in the woodlands and fields surrounding our hillside home, building camps, digging holes, kicking leaves. Cuckoos would cuckoo, owls would hoot, we'd run through hedges and hop over fences. No one cared about boundaries when our imaginations raced for miles around.

Connections with nature enfolded us. My dad would take us to collect wild watercress from streams, and we'd encourage our mum to go faster on woodland walks to spot badgers in their setts (we never did). I'll always remember the awe of seeing glow-worms (*Lampyris noctiluca*) in the churchyard next door, passers-by oblivious to our magical friends.

Life led me to London, where, despite its preponderance of brick and concrete, I noticed fragments of nature in the weeds along pavements and wildlife on derelict ground, all pointing me to a future I'd not yet realised.

Exploring wild areas in cities or the countryside can teach you so much about ecosystems and the conditions plants naturally thrive in. So much of my gardening knowledge has come from observing the wild.

Connect with the wild for your wellbeing

Although I treasure my garden, I still love escaping to the countryside, the more remote the better, where nature is free and untamed. It's where I feel free too, to explore, to be myself, to find myself again when life leaves me feeling lost. Many other people feel the same way, and our instincts are backed up by a growing body of scientific research that shows nature can heal our bodies and minds.

Doses of nature

A 2019 survey of 19,806, people published in *Scientific Reports*, showed that spending any amount of time in nature led to improvements in participants' wellbeing, but the optimum time was around 120 minutes per week. That could come from a single two-hour walk at the weekend or shorter periods spread through the week. This time in nature has interlinked psychological and physical benefits.

Psychological benefits

Nature helps our minds in a variety of ways: by giving us something calm and beautiful to look at, by distracting us, by helping us relax and by getting us away from elements of our lives that have a negative impact. A review by the UK government body Natural England in 2016 listed the following mental-health benefits of nature-based interventions:

+ Reduce stress and anxiety
+ Improve mood
+ Improve concentration and attention
+ Aid cognitive restoration
+ Increase our general perception of wellbeing
+ Improve dementia-related symptoms
+ Help manage mood disorders

Opposite If we think of gardens as places to unwind and observe plants and wildlife, rather than an endless list of jobs, anywhere can be thought of as our garden to enjoy – such as this marshland with heathers, rushes and calming ponds.

Physical benefits

I have an aversion to exercise, which isn't great because being inactive is less healthy. According to a study by Nazmi Sari (*Health Economics* 18: 8, 2009), on average an inactive person spends 38 per cent more days in hospital than an active person. It's not that I dislike exercise – I enjoy it when I find it happening to me – but I can safely say I have never once felt excited enough about going for a run to get up off the sofa and do it.

But I will always be lured out of the front door by the prospect of a walk to see beautiful views, spot an animal or catch an exciting plant in flower. Whether you're like me or you are a keen sportsperson, the wild gives us one extra reason to be physically active.

To find the best wild spots does usually require a high level of activity, walking long distances and going up and down steep hills, even wild swimming for the hardiest among us. This is all great news for our physical health; climbing up hills especially gets our blood pumping.

Of course, not only does a love of wild places lead to a physically healthier lifestyle, but being physically healthy is proven to improve our mental health too. We know from decades of research that physical exercise reduces stress, for example.

A moment of solitude

Going outside for walks, to exercise or just sit surrounded by nature offers a unique escape. Whatever has happened with friends, family, our partner or at work, time alone in nature can afford us space to think through problems or make plans for the future.

Nature does not judge us, and this is something I find particularly important when negative feelings build up. It allows us to gain a sense of perspective. When I've been at my lowest, I've gone for long walks in the countryside to look out across views stretching for miles, looked up at towering trees or the open sky, reminding me that I am but one small part of an immense universe. It helps me untangle my thoughts.

Opposite, top Wild fern, *Blechnum spicant*.
Opposite, bottom Seal pups keeping a watchful eye.

Quality time with friends and family

On the other hand, because going out into nature is largely an active pastime – walking, running, cycling – we often do it with friends or family. It can focus our social time by removing distractions (I'm looking at you, mobile phones). It's quite hard to walk along hillside paths looking out for wildlife while checking notifications and emails. Many of my most memorable times with my partner Chris have been on long walks, taking everything in together. We talk for longer and in more depth, enjoying and sharing the experience we are building with each other.

Building new friendships

Nature can help us build new friendships too. There are many opportunities to volunteer alongside like-minded people to help in wildlife reserves and urban green spaces, from litter-picking to repairing paths. A report by the New Economics Foundation in 2008 found that cooperation and working with others can increase neuronal responses in the reward areas of our brains, indicating that we find social cooperation rewarding.

Equip yourself

If you want to delve deeper into the natural world, to witness and learn its best-kept secrets, having some basic equipment with you will help. Besides the list below, there are a couple of commonsense things to do before you venture out: check the weather and take a map – there may not be any phone signal, so download one beforehand or take a paper one.

✛ **Field guides:** despite having the internet at our fingertips, detailed plant and wildlife field guidebooks or leaflets are still the best resource for accurate identification. You'd need to carry an entire library of books to cover everything you're likely to see. Instead, choose one or two field guides to carry; for everything else take photos on the day for identifying when you're home.

✛ **Folding pocket magnifying glass:** plants and insects have so much amazing detail on a microscopic level that it would be a shame to miss it.

✛ **Insect and butterfly net:** specially made, very soft nets for catching insects, which can be more closely inspected when transferred to a jar.

✛ **Insect jar with breathing holes:** there are many lightweight plastic insect jars, but to avoid plastic, I just take a small, robust jam jar. Poke a few breathing holes into the metal lid to prevent the insect from suffocating. Popping an insect into a jar allows you to take a really close look without harming it. I only keep the insect in the jar momentarily, before releasing it where I found it.

✛ **Smartphone:** in the wild I set my phone to flight mode so I'm not interrupted by phone calls, but I do always take it with me, and not just in case I fall down a ravine. It is invaluable for taking photos and searching for plant or wildlife identifications. I use the Google app reverse image search to help identify species that are new to me, and I use the location data on photos to keep a record of where I have been.

✛ **Binoculars:** described with two numbers (mine are 10 x 50): the first is the magnification power, 10 indicating that the binoculars will make an object appear ten times closer compared to the naked eye, which is good for looking at birds and wildlife. The second number is the diameter of the objective lens: the larger the number, the wider the field of vision.

✛ **Camera (not shown):** if you can afford one, it's always worth taking a good camera with you to capture particularly interesting nature finds.

Open your eyes to nature

Whenever I go for a walk in the wild, I see and experience the world in two ways. In one way I'm walking through our familiar world, concentrating on where we're going, aware of the views and life around us but ultimately passing through it. The other way of seeing the world I can describe only as pure magic, where paying enough attention opens up a true connection with the millions of interactions happening around us.

Truly seeing our world

Unfortunately for us, so much of nature has evolved to remain hidden in order to protect itself. Many wild orchids, for example autumn lady's tresses (*Spiranthes spiralis*), are tiny, blending perfectly with their grass partners; and creatures such as owls have feathers that are designed to camouflage them. 'Getting your eye in' means stopping and concentrating carefully to spot the wildlife and plants hiding from us. But this phrase doesn't capture the magical feeling of what actually happens. To me it is about tuning our senses to tap into an ability we've forgotten how to use, allowing us to open a door to nature's hidden world. Our senses become so connected to everything going on around, that we become sensitive to the ecosystem's interactions and inhabitants, and more adept at picking out what it is we are looking for.

How to tune your senses

+ **Pause:** stand still or sit down; don't move for a number of minutes, but let the world move around you.
+ **Listen:** in nature, even when it's quiet there are thousands of sounds – the wind making different trees sway and creak, bird calls, insect buzzes, leaves rustling. You may find it helps to close your eyes to concentrate on listening.
+ **Observe:** watch as the clouds travel and change, as leaves and branches sway in the wind, as birds and insects fly past. Look at the way light falls on plants in different ways; some leaves are shiny, others dull and matt. Are there slight differences in natural patterns that give away the presence of an animal?
+ **Smell:** what can you smell? A woodland can smell musty and leafy, hedgerows and meadows fresh or floral. You may smell less pleasant things like the musk of foxes and deer hides. You might smell poo ... which in itself is a kind of encounter: the animal responsible may still be close!

✛ **Touch:** it's best not to touch most wildlife because we could hurt insects and animals or damage fragile plants. However, it is good to feel different soils, to touch the different textures in bark and the strength of trunks and branches. Plants that seem similar, such as grass species, can look the same but feel different, with softer or coarser leaves.

Always respect nature
As exciting as it is to take a photo of a rare wildflower or animal, I never want to disturb them or their habitats. I once saw someone photographing a rare butterfly while simultaneously crushing the threatened flowers it needs to survive, in order to get the shot. Our footsteps can damage plant shoots, stems and roots, and our presence can scare animals away, sometimes from their young. If you can't take a photo from a safe position, it's better to enjoy the moment from a distance.

Plan what you want to see

It's possible to step out into the wild and appreciate random encounters. However, if you have a particular interest, and want to find a certain plant species in flower or see a particular insect, animal or bird, it's important to be more targeted. Perseverance pays off; if you don't see what you're looking for it doesn't mean it isn't there, so try again another day. Nature reserves usually list the species present, and you can use field guides to narrow your search area using these questions:

✛ Where are they geographically?
✛ What habitat are they found in? Grassland, woodland, scrubland, wetland or water?
✛ Is this on a particular type of soil? Alkaline chalk, acidic peatland, stony, sandy, clay or loam?
✛ Are there plants they're usually seen alongside? Perhaps used for food.
✛ Are they in shade or sun?
✛ Do they live at high or low altitudes?
✛ What time of year are they active and visible? Some flowers and insects may only be around for a matter of weeks.
✛ Does time of day matter? Wildlife is often more noticeable at dawn or dusk, while some flowers open wider or attract more insects only in strong sunlight.

Things to do in the wild

Observing nature and immersing yourself in it can be very rewarding, but there are also fun and simple activities to try out to add another dimension to your time in the wild. Here are a few things to do when you're out on your next nature jaunt.

Collect some natural treasures

When you're out and about in nature, occasionally you'll stumble across objects lying around that are particularly beautiful or captivating, such as feathers, leaves, acorns, conkers, seed heads and shells. These are nature's treasures, discarded by whichever animal or plant created them but wonderful it's wonderful to collect a couple of mementoes from your adventures. There are as many things to catch our eye as there are days to find them.

Get creative with nature art

It's easy to make designs using leaves by laying them out in circles, squares, stars or triangles, on a large scale or small – depending on how much time you have. British artist Andy Goldsworthy creates beautiful and thoughtful site-specific sculptures using pebbles, leaves and branches which you could look to for inspiration. When we create something, our minds set aside other thoughts in order to concentrate on the matter at hand. Nature art is a wonderful way to anchor ourselves in the moment and appreciate the breadth of materials

we have to create with. Autumn's a particularly good time to indulge your inner artist thanks to the volume, range and colour of leaves blanketing the ground, alongside berries and nuts.

Making nature art is a great activity to try with other people, especially young children. Here are some ideas to try:

✛ abstract shapes with no meaning
✛ patterns like circles, zig-zags, stripes, wavy lines and checks
✛ faces of people who mean something to you
✛ home or other special buildings
✛ animals
✛ trees
✛ landscapes

Opposite, top left Arrange natural objects into patterns to create fleeting works of art.
Opposite, top right The textured bark on this ancient tree is covered in moss.
Opposite, bottom Collect a few interesting objects and take them home for a closer look.

Climb trees

As a child I would climb the old yew tree in our back garden at the top of the slope. Up there I could sit securely, high in the branches, looking out across distant views, hidden from the world below. We're never too old to climb trees, so why let children have all the fun?

Safety first

Climbing trees is, of course, done at your own risk, and care must be taken to avoid slips, falls and damage to the trees themselves. With that warning out of the way, let's get climbing!

How to climb

There are three rules. First, only climb trees strong enough to take your weight without causing damage (to the tree, not you). Second, don't climb if you're feeling unwell or aren't physically agile. Third, be sure you can climb back down by carefully thinking through the route before you go up. It's no good climbing to the top of a tree and enjoying the view if, when you're finished, you find yourself stuck up there.

Why climb trees?

Better to ask, why not? We love climbing trees as children, but at some point it becomes socially unacceptable and I don't know why. Sure, it may look odd when a fully grown person climbs a tree in a park, but it's everyone else who's missing out.

Climbing a tree is fun. You don't have to climb very high. Up one branch is enough, sitting off the ground with your legs dangling, looking out across the land from a different vantage point. The daring among us will venture higher, and eventually you may get lost in the leaves, hidden in a secret world of green.

In higher branches the best views can be found and the blanket of leaves places a strange hush on the world, as if it's muffled below. It's incredibly peaceful. You might even be joined by a bird or squirrel – just don't let them scare you into losing your grip.

When I'm in the wild, I'll usually climb a tree or two, at least a little, to help experience that area better. And when I revisit the same tree, it's like revisiting an old friend, as I'm more familiar with its branches and the routes up and down.

Opposite See the world from a different perspective by climbing sturdy trees – but be careful not to damage the tree or yourself!

Explore the urban wilderness

There are plenty of interesting plants and wildlife to be found in a city or town if you look in the right places. Urban parks, commons and waste grounds are those right places.

Parks and commons

As a garden designer I've learned a great deal from exploring parks and commons in cities around the world. It can be extremely useful to see what's growing well in local parks, which have the same conditions as our garden. I grow *Cyclamen* and *Linaria purpurea* because I saw them growing well in a park a few minutes away.

Parks are more manicured than commons, designed for the needs of humans and likely to have ornamental areas planted by teams of volunteers, filled with fascinating exotic plants. Most of them have been designed and can teach us a lot about garden layouts, furniture, materials and other style decisions. Some parks have experts in horticulture and ecology on their teams, and I've learned my most important lessons from what they've done, even finding out who those people are and asking them directly! I first learned the name of *Cephalaria gigantea* after seeing it in a park before seeking out the head gardener, who was able to satisfy my curiosity.

Commons, on the other hand, are semi-wild land where wildflowers, shrubs and wildlife run free. Decisions on what to grow are ecologically led, except where land is used for sports, helping protect wild plants, insects and animals. It's on commons that I've learned which insects are drawn to certain wildflowers, from butterflies on thistles and flat-topped *Achillea millefolium*, to bumblebees on teasels and foxgloves.

Waste grounds

I must make a special mention of waste grounds in urban areas, abandoned patches of land forgotten by humans but repopulated by wildlife. These are often called brownfield sites because they used to have buildings on them and probably will again. Waste grounds are filled with plants that many people see as weeds, but these tough wildflowers can teach us a lot about the types of plant that like to grow naturally in harsh urban conditions.

Opposite, top Orange *Tithonia rotundifolia* glow in the Old English garden at Battersea Park, London, by designer Sarah Price.
Opposite, bottom Alliums and poppies bring colour to concrete at the Barbican in London, reimagined by designer Nigel Dunnett.

Urban landscape lessons

Walk around every part of a park or common and ask yourself...

✛ What plants are growing?

✛ How well are plants growing together? Do any combinations look better than others?

✛ What are the conditions they're growing in? Sun or shade, dry soil or damp?

✛ Which are in flower, and which will flower later or have done so already?

✛ What insects or animals do you see on them?

✛ Why are different types of wildlife drawn to different plants?

✛ What materials are used for patios and paths?

✛ Which plants and wildlife are other people drawn to? Why do you think that is?

✛ How have things changed when you revisit in a different season?

Visit other people's gardens

Until I became fully immersed in the world of gardening, I didn't realise visiting other people's private gardens was a done thing. But around the world people open their gardens to the public, often to raise money for charity, and it's one of the best ways of gaining new ideas and inspiration while meeting like-minded people.

Local open days

Nowadays, Chris and I check online to see if there are any nearby private gardens open at weekends or wherever we are on holiday. The variety of garden types, sizes and styles is limitless and you never know what to expect, from traditional to tropical, naturalistic to formal.

In towns and cities where gardens are smaller, there's always a little awkward moment when you first arrive at the door, hand over a donation and find yourself making small talk with people. Then you realise everyone is lovely and knowledgeable about what they've grown, including what hasn't worked.

Sharing experiences with people in similar gardens to yours is invaluable; their advice can save you years of trial and error. Seeing plants at first hand, rather than in glossy magazines and online, helps you to understand how plants grow and to what size.

From a wellbeing point of view, visiting a garden for an hour or two beats going to the shops or watching TV, keeping you active in the fresh air. I consider the experience as enriching as visiting art galleries. A private garden is a living creation full of the personality of the gardener.

When I first started gardening in London I thought I was the only person who did. Now I'm surrounded by good friends I've met through visiting gardens locally and further afield. Chris and I even ended up opening our garden as part of the UK's National Garden Scheme, helping to raise over £5,000 for their charity beneficiaries.

Oh, and did I mention there is almost always cake?

Opposite, top A relaxed naturalistic scheme of soft greens and purples brings a feeling of enclosure to this private seating space.
Opposite, bottom Garden designer Miria Harris has cleverly incorporated perceived weed flowers to the grass and lets it grow in front of a studio and dining spot.

Rewild gardens, streets and verges

As our urban sprawl increases, it's important to help nature exist alongside us, for our own sake as much as for nature's. Acting now to understand how nature can be included in cities and towns will help species survive and bring us the benefits of living closer to the wild. It's one of the most important things we can do right now.

Street plants are essential for wildlife

There is far less diversity of wildlife in urban areas than rural areas. We don't need research to prove that, we see it with our own eyes. Roads, walls, buildings and fences block access for wildlife to move around, and cement and stone reduce the space for plants for food and shelter. We can each help counter this with a few small actions.

Grow more street trees

In a world of constant development, the value of trees in cities and towns cannot be overstated. On a street with a road and pavements, trees may be the only plants growing. Trees improve the appearance of streets, help to trap pollution on leaves, and provide fantastic food and habitat for birds, bats and insects. You can contact your local authority to make sure no spots for trees go unused and to encourage them to choose the right trees for your area. Trees indigenous to

Above Trees in Bonnington Square, London, add huge plant mass for birds and insects. Residents have underplanted them with shrubs and perennials to create a green, inviting oasis in the city for both humans and wildlife.

your region are always a great choice for local wildlife, and I'm a huge fan of fruit trees, which provide beautiful blossom in spring that turns to fruit for residents and wildlife to eat in autumn and winter. Many people are put off by the mess of the fruit if it's left unused, but I believe this is shortsighted and misses a huge opportunity to taste local free food.

Plant under street trees

On the road parallel to ours in London, local residents have for a decade worked with our local council to allow the wild plants under the trees to grow freely. Usually plants growing in soil beneath street trees are called weeds and blitzed with weedkillers, which obviously isn't good practice. We've grown up in a society that told us neat and tidy and weed-free is good for us, but we know now that the opposite is true. Wildlife and plants make us feel better and street plants are another great micro-habitat for wildlife. You can plant flowers you like beneath street trees too, but please make sure they are wildlife-friendly ones.

Let verges grow wild

Verges along roads and train tracks act as vital habitat for wildflowers, insects and animals. In fact, they're some of the only truly wild places in cities and towns because we don't really care for them – except when they are mown short for tidiness. Mown verges are almost as lifeless as the pavements next to them. Verges cover large areas and can be treated like a meadow, filled with colourful wildflowers for pollinators and other insects, and requiring less maintenance. If safety for vehicles is important, a 20–30cm (8–12in) mown strip next to the road is an acceptable compromise. Wild verges act as wildlife corridors, linking larger parks and other green spaces like gardens – important because many insects can't actually fly or crawl very far.

Over to you

I love our garden on Littlebury Road. It's our space; me, Chris and Rumbles. Though small, it offers more than enough room to satisfy my gardening mind. Slowly nurturing nature is a powerful way to help manage my stress and anxiety.

My hope is that this book helps you connect with nature in your own way. We're all different and our growing spaces reflect that, be it garden, balcony or window boxes.

At the same time, we can't escape the damage we are causing to the garden we all share: the wild. Nature needs true wild expanses, and while our gardens help, we can't keep taking land for ourselves. Nature will only survive if it has its own home. Protecting the last fragments of wild habitat is one of our biggest responsibilities, and this includes giving land back, enlarging wilderness for species to survive. This act simultaneously locks atmospheric carbon into plant life and soil and helps to slow climate change.

We're part of the natural world and to save it is to save ourselves. We all benefit from a greener life.

A rough guide to the year

Always check guidance for your specific plants, because they all vary, but here are a few basics to keep in mind.

Winter

This is when plant growth slows to a standstill, leaves fall and plants die back, protected against the cold, wet and windy weather below ground. Insects shelter in a state of diapause and bats hibernate. Use this time for planning, cleaning and dreaming of the year to come. And get out into the wild to look for shoots and other signs of spring to come.

- ✛ Feed birds, clean bird boxes.
- ✛ Leave seed heads for wildlife.
- ✛ Break ice for wildlife to drink.
- ✛ Plant bare-root fruit trees and bushes.
- ✛ Prune apples and pears (leave cherries and plums until mid-summer).
- ✛ Prune deciduous climbers including clematis, wisteria and climbing roses.
- ✛ Prune roses, buddleia, sambucus and other late summer-flowering shrubs if advised.
- ✛ Repot house plants.
- ✛ Plan for the year ahead, ordering seeds and plants.

Spring

Buds and bulbs hunkering down in winter burst open and grow rapidly with lush leaves and bright flowers. This is the busiest season of the year for the gardener, sowing seeds and planting new plants. Wildlife can be seen in abundance as birds start nesting, insects and mammals mating. The first wildflowers line hedgerows and meadows.

- ✛ In very early spring, cut back dead perennial growth to make room for for spring bulbs and new growth.
- ✛ In late spring cut some perennials back by 50% to promote branching and more flowers.
- ✛ Add 2–3cm (about 1in) mulch if not added in autumn.
- ✛ Divide grasses and other perennials.
- ✛ Plant new plants outdoors.
- ✛ Sow hardy annual flowers outside.
- ✛ Sow tomatoes indoors in early spring for extra growing time.
- ✛ Sow seeds of most vegetables in mid-spring as the days grow longer.
- ✛ Plant potatoes.
- ✛ Prune warmer-climate shrubs including salvias, rosemary and penstemon.
- ✛ Evergreen shrubs that can be trimmed should be now.

Summer	Autumn

After the rush of spring, summer is a season of exuberance and relaxation, with fewer jobs but more to enjoy. Spring bulbs and blossoms are overtaken by summer perennials and shrubs. Go for long evening walks to spot wildlife and wildflowers. Eat outside to enjoy bees and hoverflies surrounded by colour!

Leaves change colour alongside late-flowering plants for an incredibly beautiful last hurrah complemented by berries, colchicum, *Cyclamen hederifolum* and nerines. Fungi can be seen on walks in the wet, warm conditions. Harvests are abundant as veg plots and orchards hit their peak. Birds migrate or shelter in gardens.

Summer

+ Dead-head repeat-flowering plants such as dahlias, rudbeckia, helenium and roses.
+ Plant veg and flower seedlings outside when large enough and all risk of frost has passed.
+ Start watering pot plants regularly and feed with seaweed or homemade fertiliser every couple of weeks.
+ Continuously sow seeds of fast-growing vegetables, such as salad leaves, radish and spring onion.
+ Sow seeds of slower-growing vegetables every six weeks or so for successive crops, such as peas, beans and Florence fennel.
+ Prune cherries and plums.
+ Support floppy plants.
+ Collect seeds as they ripen (and in autumn).
+ Prune early-flowering shrubs and climbers.

Autumn

+ Plant bulbs toward the end of autumn as the weather turns cold.
+ In early autumn take cuttings.
+ Divide perennials (leave grasses until spring) and replant.
+ Top up planting areas with a 2–3cm (about 1in) mulch of compost or well-rotted manure, keeping it away from plant stems.
+ Give hedges a final clip before winter to keep them tidy.
+ Store produce for winter, such as squash. Dry chillies, tomatoes, herbs and beans. Freeze fresh greens.
+ Sow winter salads, peas and broad beans.
+ Plant garlic.

Glossary

Annual: a plant that grows, sets seed and dies in one year.

Anxiety: feelings of worry or fear that can be mild or build up. It is normal for people to feel anxious at times, but when it starts to affect your life it's worth speaking to someone about it.

Biennial: a plant that grows in its first year, then flowers, sets seed and dies the second year.

Biological: relating to something that is or was alive (e.g. compost made from plants).

Bulb: fleshy underground leaves that protect a new stem and store food for the plant.

Compost: decomposed plant matter used as a medium for growing other plants.

Cultivars: plants that do not appear naturally in the wild, but are bred by people.

Cuttings: stems or leaves cut from a plant with the intention of rooting them in water or compost.

Decay: see Decomposition

Decomposition: the process of dead plant or animal matter breaking down, often by fungi and microorganisms.

Diversity: a mix of different varieties of plants and wildlife.

Ecology: study of the way living organisms interact with one another and their environment.

Ecosystem: plants and wildlife living in the same location that form a network of interaction they're dependent on to survive.

Environment: the conditions in an area created by soil, plants and climate (i.e. weather, temperature and seasons). Can relate to a small space, visible vistas or vast areas such as an entire continent.

Exotic: a plant or animal that originates in a distant country and has unusual characteristics compared to local indigenous species.

Grasses: family of plants called Poaceae that are all wind-pollinated and have narrow leaves and rounded hollow stems called culms.

Groundcover: low-growing plants that spread outwards to completely cover the soil.

Habitat: an area of land or water in which plants and wildlife live.

Hardiness: describes how tolerant a plant is of cold and wet conditions. Minimum temperature tolerance is rated on a scale of H1 (5°C or higher) to H7 (-20°C or lower) in the UK, or the reverse in the USA: Z1 (-60°F) to Z13 (70°F).

Herb: for cooking this is a term to describe plants used as an ingredient to flavour food or drinks; for botany it is used to mean Herbaceous (see below).

Herbaceous: a plant that has no woody stem, often but not always dying back once a year.

Hybrid: the offspring of two plants with different characteristics, usually from different species.

Indigenous: evolved naturally without human intervention in a particular area or region.

Organic: something that is or was once alive; or grown naturally without chemicals.

Organic matter: growing media consisting of once living material, e.g. plant-based compost and well-rotted manure.

Ornamental: a decorative plant, i.e. not planted for food or other practical purpose.

Peat: dead plant material that has only partially decomposed due to unique acidic waterlogged conditions of bogs. Formed over millennia, peat bogs are one of the planet's largest carbon stores and cannot be classed as renewable.

Perennial: living for several years.

Propagate: to grow new plants, such as from seed, cuttings or division.

Psychology: scientific understanding of how the mind works.

Rewild: to return land to its natural state, with no or minimal input from humans.

Rhizomes: roots that spread horizontally underground, developing new shoots along them.

Runner: see Stolons.

Seed: structure containing fertilised ovules of a plant; an embryonic plant.

Senescence: the period when a plant or part of its structure begins to deteriorate or die.

Stolons: above-ground shoots that usually grow horizontally with roots and shoots growing along them creating new plants. Also called runners.

Stress: our body's reaction to feeling under pressure or threatened.

Sustainable: won't run out or can be renewed.

Tuber: thickened part of a stem or rhizome found underground (e.g. potatoes and dahlias).

Variety (var.): plants in a species with naturally occurring differences (e.g. rounded vs elongated leaves).

Weeds: an unwanted plant that reproduces seemingly uncontrollably.

Wellbeing: the state of being comfortable, healthy, or happy.

Wild/wilderness: areas of land or water largely untouched by human activity.

Wildflower: a flowering plant growing in the wild, not in gardens or parks.

Index

Page numbers in *italics* indicate illustration captions.

Acknowledgements

A Greener Life was started as the coronavirus pandemic struck and is finishing a few weeks after my vaccine. The book's creation provided a focus through tragedy and I'm personally grateful for spending time with the people who chose to work on it, despite the chaos affecting them.

Thank you Zara, Chelsea, Rachel and Zoë. Zara Larcombe for commissioning the book and helping shape its structure. My editor, Chelsea, for leading us through this marathon, improving every page. Rachel Warne for your artful photography and energy. Zoë Plant at The Bent Agency for your wisdom in setting us on this journey. Thank you to Alison Effeny for your critical eye and Sarah Pyke for your talented, beautiful design work.

Thank you to Peter and Alex Shepherd, Kathy Thompson, Lucy Lewthwaite, Emma and David Dean, and Alex Smith for your trust in me. I'd also like to thank Gina Gilbert for your front-door pots; Niwaki for a few of the tools featured; and Waterside Nursery for pond-plant advice.

I'm grateful to the people who've helped shape my gardening journey: Philip Oostenbrink, Annie Shaw, Monty Don, Joanna Fortnam, Stephen Barney, Benny Hawksbee, Alice Vincent, Claire Ratinon, Andrew O'Brien, Sue Phipps, Peter Langley, Julie Penny and the education departments at the Royal Horticultural Society and Royal Botanic Garden Edinburgh.

John and Sally-Ann Wallington for introducing us all to wild nature. Hannah and Edward Wallington and Krista McKinzey-Wallington for your support and our shared love of the wild. If you all hadn't done these things I might never have found this path.

Most importantly, thank you to my partner Christopher Lyon Anderson for your kindness, patience and encouragement. Your advice makes everything I do a collaboration with you.

Picture credits

All images courtesy of Jack Wallington, except for the following pages.

Gap Photos: GAP Photos/Jonathan Buckley – Design: Sarah Raven: 143 (bottom).

Rachel Warne: 15 (left), 17 (top), 19, 21, 26, 28, 30, 32, 35, 37, 38, 40, 41, 42, 43, 61 (top), 64 (top and middle), 65 (top and bottom right), 66, 75 (bottom), 81 (middle, left and bottom), 82, 85, 93 (top), 102, 103, 107, 109, 117 (left), 125 (top), 126, 127, 129, 132, 133, 137, 140, 143 (top), 144, 146, 148, 149, 151, 155, 157, 158, 180, 184 (top), 186 (left), 187, 192.

Shutterstock: Radka Palenikova: 17 (bottom); Alis Photo: 117 (top); Erni: 118 (top); godi photo: 118 (bottom); Miroslav Hlavko: 121.

Further reading

Designing with Grasses by Neil Lucas, 2011
Dream Plants for the Natural Garden by Piet Oudolf and Henk Gerritson, 2013
Gardening with Shape, Line, and Texture by Linden Hawthorne, 2009
Naturalistic Planting Design by Nigel Dunnett, 2019
Phytomedicines, Herbal Drugs and Poisons by Ben-Erik Van Wyk and Michael Wink, 2015
Planting in a Post-Wild World by James Rainer and Claudia West, 2015
Sowing Beauty by James Hitchmough, 2017
The Complete Gardener by Monty Don, 2021
The Garden Jungle by Dave Goulson, 2020
The Well-Gardened Mind by Sue Stuart-Smith, 2021
Wildflowers of Britain and Ireland by Marjorie Blamey, Richard Fitter and Alastair Fitter, 2013

About the author

Jack Wallington is an ecological grower and landscape designer who's created over 70 gardens, from tiny city balconies to country estates, specialising in modern gardens with regenerative, wildlife-friendly planting. He's appeared on BBC *Gardeners' World* and writes for *The Guardian*, *The Telegraph*, *Gardens Illustrated*, RHS's *The Garden* and others. His book *Wild about Weeds: Garden Design with Rebel Plants* was named Gardening Book of the Year by *The Times* in 2019.